The Days of Dylan Thomas

Southwest Wales

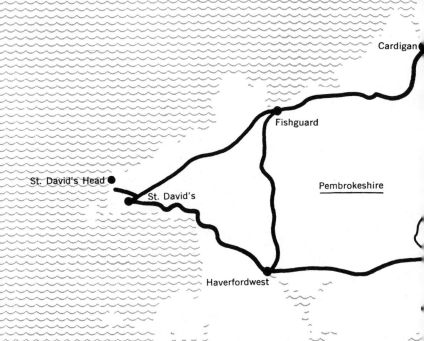

Cardigan

Fishguard

St. David's Head

St. David's

Pembrokeshire

Haverfordwest

Tenby

The Days of Dylan Thomas

By Bill Read
With photographs by
Rollie McKenna
and others

McGraw-Hill Book Company   New York   Toronto   London

Acknowledgments

Like every author, I am deeply indebted for help that cannot be adequately acknowledged. I am particularly grateful for the kindnesses of Caitlin Thomas, Yvonne Macnamara, Pamela Hansford Johnson, A. E. Trick, John Malcolm Brinnin, and Kent E. Thompson.

A number of people in Wales were extraordinarily generous to me, chief among whom were Ronald Cour, Aneirin Talfan Davies, Gweveril Brace Dawkins, Gwynfor Evans, Rene Harding, Alfred Janes, Emrys Jones, Morley Jones, Ellis Lloyd, Christina March, Dr. Thomas Parry, Leslie M. Rees, Philip Richards, Margaret Anne Rogers, Ethel Ross, A. E. Savage, G. Froom Tyler, Gwen and Vernon Watkins and Ivy Williams.

Friends of the poet in England who were equally generous included Sydney Box, John Davenport, T. S. Eliot, Sir Arthur Elton, William Empson, Constantine FitzGibbon, Geoffrey Grigson, Wyn Henderson, David Higham, Mervyn Levy, Jack Lindsay, Cordelia Locke, Elisabeth Lutyens, Brigit Marnier, Bert Newlands, Roland Penrose, Keidrych Rhys, A. J. P. Taylor, and Donald Taylor. There was further help from Ruth Witt-Diamant in Tokyo, from Roberto Sanesi in Milan, and from Evgeni Evtushenko in Moscow.

And in America I am grateful for the special help of William Abrahams, Gertrude Buckman, Robert Craft, Elizabeth Reitell Hannum, Jutta Heyne, James Laughlin IV, Marianne Mantell, Ralph Maud, Howard Moss, William Moynihan, Mary Golden Read, F. W. Roberts, and John L. Sweeney.

For permission to reprint copyright material the thanks of the author and publisher are offered the following:

Adam International Review for passages by Pamela Hansford Johnson, Elisabeth Lutyens, Mario Luzi, Runia Sheila MacLeod, and Dylan Thomas (Nos. 236 and 238 [1953]).

The Adelphi for passages by Rayner Heppenstall (Feb., 1935) and John Arlott (Vol. 30, No. 2 [1954]).

Books for passages by E. F. Bozman (Dec., 1953).

British Broadcasting Corporation for passages by Edwin Muir, The Listener (Feb. 27, 1935).

J. M. Dent & Sons, Ltd., New Directions, and the Dylan Thomas Literary Executors for passages by Dylan Thomas, Quite Early One Morning (1954), Under Milk Wood (1954), Letters to Vernon Watkins (1957), and Collected Poems (1952).

J. M. Dent & Sons, Ltd., for passages from Ralph

Maud and Aneirin Talfan Davies, eds., The Colour of Saying (1963).

Encounter for passages by Daniel Jones, Louis MacNeice, and Vernon Watkins (Jan., 1954, and Feb., 1956).

John O'London's for passages by Mervyn Levy (Nov. 29, 1962).

Little, Brown and Co.–Atlantic Monthly Press and J. M. Dent & Sons, Ltd., for passages from Dylan Thomas in America copyright 1955 by John Malcolm Brinnin.

London Magazine for passages by Geoffrey Grigson (Sept., 1957).

New American Library of World Literature, Inc., for passages by Dylan Thomas, New World Writing No. 7 (April, 1955).

New Directions for six poems from The Collected Poems of Dylan Thomas, copyright 1953 by Dylan Thomas, © 1957 by New Directions, reprinted by permission of New Directions.

Poetry and Mrs. Roy Campbell for passages by Roy Campbell (Nov., 1955).

Putnam & Co., Ltd., for passages from Caitlin Thomas' Leftover Life to Kill (1957).

Jan Read and Thomas Nelson and Sons for passages from an unpublished introduction to The Beach of Falesa.

South Wales Evening Post for passages from the issues of June 2, 1931, and others.

Swansea Grammar School Magazine (Dec., 1925) and Adam International Review (No. 238 [1953]) for "Song of a Mischievous Dog."

The Texas Quarterly for passages by Dylan Thomas (Vol. IV, No. 4 [Winter, 1961]).

The Dylan Thomas Literary Executors for passages by Dylan Thomas quoted from magazines no longer extant.

Times Literary Supplement (London) for passages from a review of Twenty-Five Poems (Sept. 19, 1936).

I am indebted to three libraries for their generous help: the Swansea Public Library, the Houghton Library of Harvard University, and (particularly for the letters to Pamela Hansford Johnson) the Lockwood Memorial Library of the University of New York at Buffalo.

Contents

15	Chronology
21	The Beginning
24	Cwmdonkin Park
26	The Schoolboy
35	The Reporter
45	The Young Poet
50	The Actor
53	The Prize Winner
55	Pamela Hansford Johnson
70	In Chelsea
79	In Donegal
82	Surrealism
84	Caitlin Macnamara
91	In Wales
100	War Years
102	The Malting House
103	Documentary Films
113	Craftsmanship
115	Radio Work
119	Bohemianism
123	In Italy
125	In Oxfordshire
127	Feature Films
133	In Prague; Politics
137	In America
144	In Laugharne
152	In America II
159	In America III
167	The End
178	Concerning The Names
179	Sources of Quotations
182	Bibliography
185	Index

The Photographs

2   Diagram map of Southwest Wales
18 Tidal beach at the Boat House
20 Rhossilli Bay, Gower Peninsula
20 Cwmdonkin Drive, Mumbles in distance
23 David John Thomas, c. 1900
23 Florence Williams Thomas, c. 1934
23 Paraclete Congregational Church, Newton, Mumbles
25 Dylan and Mother at Fern Hill, 1952
25 Barnyard at Fern Hill
27 The right half of this house is No. 5 Cwmdonkin Drive, Dylan's childhood home
27 Upper slope of Cwmdonkin Park
27 The view from Dylan's room
30 Dylan's first published poem
30 Dylan in September, 1925
33 Diagram map of Swansea
36 Dylan and his mother
37 The newspaper office
37 Article from the Herald of Wales
39 Dylan, c. 1938
43 Fountain in the Park
43 Cwmdonkin Park bandstand
46 Dylan
49 The Worm's Head, Gower Peninsula
49 Bert and Nell Trick at Caswell Bay, Gower
56 Manuscript of "The Force that Through the Green Fuse"
64 Pamela Hansford Johnson, c. 1936
64 A photograph given by Dylan to Pamela, c. 1935
64 Pamela Hansford Johnson, Aunt Pollie, Mrs. Thomas, Uncle Dai and Aunt Dosie Rees, Uncle Bob, 1936
73 Mervyn Levy by Alfred Janes
73 Dylan by Alfred Janes
77 Edith Sitwell
77 Dylan's doodle of Sitwell and Moore
83 Garden of Richard Hughes' home by Laugharne Castle
86 Eurhythmic dancing by Caitlin
86 Caitlin Macnamara by Augustus John
86 Home of Yvonne Macnamara, Blashford, Ringwood
88 Dylan and Caitlin

89 "In loving memory of Annie Jones, Mount Pleasant, Llangain, died 7 Feb. 1933, 70 years old. Also her husband James Jones, died 3 Sept. 1942, 78 years old."

89 Dylan and his mother at Mount Pleasant

89 Dylan and Caitlin

93 Sea View, Laugharne

93 Laugharne Main Street

93 Vernon Watkins by Alfred Janes

94 Dylan and Caitlin

94 Croquet at Vernon Watkins', Pennard Cliffs, Gower

97 Diagram map of Laugharne

99 Llewelyn and parents

99 Dylan by Augustus John

105 "I walked abroad in a shower of all my days"

105 Baby Aeron and parents

108 "With water praying and call of seagull and rook"

112 "On the hill's shoulder . . . the wood faraway under me"

114 With Patric Dickinson, head of BBC poetry programs, 1946

114 Dylan doodles

118 Poetry reading on the Third Programme

118 Vernon Watkins, John Prichard, Fred Janes, John Griffiths, Dan Jones, Dylan Thomas, Oct. 24, 1949

120 The Mandrake Club, Soho

120 Dylan by Michael Ayrton

121 The Savage Club, Carleton House Terrace

121 "The ranks of regularly conducted society"

126 Dylan

126 The Boat House on the Taf Estuary, Laugharne

130 "Milk Wood" (Laugharne) and Sir John's Hill

135 Playing Nap with Ebbie and Ivy Williams

135 Dylan by Mervyn Levy

135 "One front tooth broken after playing a game called Cats and Dogs in the Mermaid, Mumbles"

138 John Malcolm Brinnin

142 Dylan, Billy Williams, Caitlin, and Bill Read at St. David's, Pembroke

142 Dylan's Shack on Cliff Walk

143 Caitlin with Aeron and Colm

145 Colm Garan Thomas

145 The Thomases at St. David's

145 The family
147 Notes for "Poem on His Birthday"
148 Manuscript of "Do Not Go Gentle"
151 Dylan
154 Chelsea Hotel, New York
154 Caitlin's caricature of Dylan
154 Dylan with small cigar
158 Llewelyn Edouard Thomas
158 Aeron Thomas
161 Citizens of Laugharne
161 At the bar of the White Horse Tavern
162 Elizabeth Reitell
162 Citizens of Laugharne
162 Cast of Under Milk Wood
165 Reading poetry
168 Directing Under Milk Wood
168 "Guilt and grief and illness"
169 "I've lived with it a long time and know it horridly well and can't explain it"
171 Caitlin
171 Caitlin, the widow
172 St. Martin's Churchyard, Laugharne
172 Welsh farmland
174 "Time has ticked a heaven round the stars"
177 Dylan
177 Welsh countryside

Credits for Photographs

All photographs in this book were taken by Rollie McKenna with the following exceptions:

Chronology

October 27, 1914	Born in Swansea, South Wales
1925–1931	Educated at Swansea Grammar School
1931–1932	Worked for the South Wales Daily Post
1930–1934	Period of greatest poetic productivity
1932–1934	Acted with the Swansea Little Theatre
May 18, 1933	First publication in New English Weekly
Sept. 3, 1933	First publication in Sunday Referee
Sept., 1933	Began correspondence with Pamela Hansford Johnson
Feb. 23, 1934	First trip to see Miss Johnson in London
Nov. 11, 1934	Moved to London
Dec. 18, 1934	Publication of 18 Poems
Summer, 1935	Vacationed in Donegal
June 26, 1936	Participated in poetry reading at the Surrealist Exhibition
Sept. 10, 1936	Twenty-Five Poems
July 12, 1937	Married Caitlin Macnamara
Oct., 1937	Moved to Ringwood, Hampshire
Aug., 1938	Moved to Sea View, Laugharne
Jan. 30, 1939	Birth of Llewelyn Thomas in Hampshire
Aug. 24, 1939	The Map of Love
Dec. 20, 1939	The World I Breathe
April 4, 1940	Portrait of the Artist as a Young Dog
Spring, 1940	Rejected for military service
June, 1940	Moved to the Malting House, Wiltshire
Fall, 1940	Moved to London
1940–1944	Wrote scenarios for documentary films
March 3, 1943	Birth of Aeron Thomas in London
Spring, 1945	Moved to New Quay, Cardiganshire
1945–1950	Wrote and performed for BBC
Feb. 7, 1946	Deaths and Entrances
Sept., 1946	Moved to Oxford
Nov. 8, 1946	The Selected Writings of Dylan Thomas
Spring, 1947	Trip to Italy
1948	Wrote feature-length films
March, 1949	Moved to the Boat House, Laugharne
March, 1949	Trip to Prague
July 24, 1949	Birth of Colm Thomas in Carmarthen
Feb. 21–May 31, 1950	First trip to America
Aug. 31, 1950	Twenty-Six Poems

Jan., 1951	Trip to Persia
Jan. 20–May 16, 1952	Second trip to America
Feb. 28, 1952	In Country Sleep
Nov. 10, 1952	Collected Poems
April 21–June 3, 1953	Third trip to America
Oct. 19, 1953	Fourth trip to America
Nov. 9, 1953	Death in New York City
Nov. 24, 1953	Burial in St. Martin's Churchyard, Laugharne

The Days of Dylan Thomas

Tidal beach at the Boat House

Rhossilli Bay, Gower Peninsula

Cwmdonkin Drive, Mumbles in distance

The Beginning

The days of Dylan Marlais Thomas began on October 27, 1914, at No. 5, Cwmdonkin Drive, Uplands, Swansea, Glamorganshire, South Wales. Swansea, he wrote, was "an ugly, lovely town (or so it was and is to me), crawling, sprawling by a long and splendid curving shore where truant boys and sandfield boys and old men from nowhere, beachcombed, idled and paddled, watched the dock-bound ships or the ships steaming away into wonder and India, magic and China, countries bright with oranges and loud with lions." Swansea was and is a lovely town with serpentine rows of houses that wind around steep hills surrounding a bay shaped like a horseshoe. In the mists and rains, it stands glistening and mysterious; when the sun comes out, the slate roofs flash with the brilliance of diamonds. Swansea is also an ugly town, often gray and black with smoke from the iron, steel, coal, and tinplate factories that spread along the east side of the River Tawe. Most of the copper works have closed down, but the biggest zinc works in Great Britain is at nearby Llansamlet and the largest oil refinery in Europe is at Llandarcy. The 160,000 natives of the port are aware that they live in a town of industrial blight. But when a Swansea man is oppressed by the grim aspects of his town he can always look to the natural paradise of the Gower Peninsula which spreads out its seventy-five square miles west into the Bristol Channel. From the famous lighthouse of Mumbles Head to the extraordinary promontory called the Worm's Head on Rhossili Bay, Gower is a region of green moors, sandy bays, crescent-shaped beaches, and spectacular bluffs which drop abruptly into the sea. At Llanrhidian stands Arthur's Stone, a dolmen fourteen feet high, one of the venerable monuments of Wales. Today this land of golden gorse, blue butterflies and sea winds remains the land of summer pleasures it was in the twenties when the boy Dylan used to run on the sands of Rhossili Bay. North from the Gower Peninsula are Carmarthen Bay, Pendine Sands, and Carmarthenshire, the home of Dylan's ancestors.

The most eminent among these was his great-uncle William Thomas, who was known by his pen name Gwilym Marles. Born in 1834, William attended a theological college in Carmarthen—entering as a Congregationalist and emerging as a Unitarian. He completed his education at the University of Glasgow, then returned to Wales to become minister of two small Unitarian churches in South Cardiganshire. He edited a magazine, Yr Athraw (The Teacher), wrote a novel for a Welsh monthly magazine, and contributed literary, religious, and political articles to Yr Ymofynydd (The Inquirer), the official Welsh Unitarian organ. A volume of his verse, Prydyddiaeth (Poetry), appeared in 1859, one poem from which is included in the current Oxford Book of Welsh Verse. In addition to his activities as a preacher and a writer, Gwilym Marles also ran a school from 1860 until his death in 1879.

Gwilym Marles' brother was Evan Thomas, the grandfather of Dylan, who settled at The Poplars in Johnstown, a suburb of Carmarthen. A guard on the Great Western Railway, Evan Thomas died in 1911—before Dylan was born. Grandpa and Grandma Evan Thomas had three sons: Arthur, William, and David John. David John, who would become Dylan's father, was the only intellectual of the three. Born in 1876, he attended the Boys' Board School in Carmarthen, where he won a Queen's Scholarship entitling him to free college tuition and a maintenance grant. He chose to attend the University College of Wales in Aberystwyth, which he entered in the fall of 1895. There he studied Latin, English, and logic, with a little French and Welsh, and prepared for a teaching career. His extracurricular activities were all musical: he was secretary of the Musical Society and leader of the Male Voice Party. In 1899 he graduated from Aberystwyth with a B.A. and first-class honors in English. He had little trouble finding a teaching position with the Swansea Grammar School, of which he eventually became Senior English Master.

In Swansea, he met Florence Williams, who had been born there in 1882. "Florrie," a bright-eyed young woman with blonde curly hair, was the daughter of a railway inspector who was also a deacon of the Swansea Canaan Congregational Church. Her brothers and sisters were to become famous as the aunts and uncles of Dylan's stories: Elizabeth Mary ("Polly") played the chapel organ; Theodosia ("Dosie") became the wife of the minister of the grim-looking Canaan chapel, Mr. David ("Dai") Rees. The Rev. Mr. Rees assisted in the ceremony at the Castle Street Congregational Church when, on December 30, 1903, David John Thomas married Florence Williams. It was to the maternal side of his family that Dylan owed his acquaintance with the Bible, for his father was not exactly sympathetic to the hard-bitten Nonconformist tradition of the Welsh countryside. Dylan was to recall his father as not so much an agnostic or an atheist as a man who had a violent and quite personal dislike for God. He would glare out the window and growl, "It's raining, blast Him!" or "The sun is shining—Lord, what foolishness!"

On the Williams side of the family there was a great

David John Thomas, c. 1900

Florence Williams Thomas,
c. 1934

Paraclete Congregational Church,
Newton, Mumbles

deal of religious activity. Dylan's grandfather was a deacon, his Uncle Tom Williams was a Swansea preacher, and his Uncle David Rees became a well-known figure as minister of the Church of the Paraclete in Newton, a position he held from 1898 until 1933. Dylan, his mother, and his older sister Nancy all attended the Congregational Church, where Dylan earned the Sunday School certificate he kept on the wall of his room. When they went to visit Aunt Dosie and Uncle Dai on week ends, as they often did, everyone went to church services three times a day at the Paraclete: morning services at eleven, Sunday school at two-thirty, and evening services at six-thirty.

The other major influence on Dylan's life from the maternal side of the family was that of farm life and the countryside. Florrie Williams and her five brothers and sisters, though born in Swansea, spent much of their time with their grandparents in the Carmarthenshire countryside—first at Waunfwlchan, Llangain, and later at Penycoed, Llangynog. The boy Dylan sometimes visited these scenes of his mother's childhood; most memorable of all, for him, were his long summer visits to his Aunt Annie and her husband Jim Jones and their son Idris (Gwilym in the story "The Peaches") who lived at a dairy farm in Llangain called Fern Hill.

Cwmdonkin Park

Few poets have been so lucky in the places they have lived. Dylan Thomas' various neighborhoods—in Swansea, in New Quay, in Laugharne—are all of spectacular natural beauty. Number 5 Cwmdonkin Drive, Swansea, where Dylan was born, has a view from its upper windows that encompasses a hillside of slate roofs descending to the sea and a panorama of the entire southern horizon —the great sweeping harbor of the town. In the east are the smokestacks of the tinplate works, in the center the docks with their cranes and wharves, in the west are the sandy swimming beaches and, finally, the punctuation point of the Mumbles Head Lighthouse. Directly in front of the house (No. 5 makes up the south half of a two-family house), is the grassed-over reservoir which is beside Cwmdonkin Park—now famous as the setting of the lyric "The Hunchback in the Park"—where the infant Dylan was wheeled in a pram and where he was taken to see the Punch and Judy: it is a public park of perhaps five acres on a precipitous hillside.

When they were young Dylan and his friends would not enter by the upper two gates or by the lower main gate to this

Dylan and Mother at Fern Hill, 1952

Barnyard at Fern Hill

"iron-railed universe," this place of "terrors and treasures." It was more fun to walk along the top of the reservoir and force a way under the wire fence that encloses the little brush forest on the east side. The most dramatic approach to the park, nevertheless, is from above. The northeast gate opens on a long flight of steeply descending, hairpin-curved, moss-covered steps that lead through a wilderness of giant evergreens and alpine growth mixed incongruously and romantically with yucca, palmetto, and monkey trees. The steep path has a sweeping view over the rooftops toward Swansea Harbor. At the west end of the park is the Rose Garden; in the center is a sweet shop, tennis courts, and a bowling green; near the entrance is the fountain and pool. The Rockery, missing for some time, has recently been restored; and the old Victorian drinking fountain with its cups hanging on a chain now has shiny faucets. In the center of the park is a large stone carved, in 1964, with the poet's words: "Oh as I was young and easy in the mercy of his means, / Time held me green and dying / Though I sang in my chains like the sea."

The Schoolboy

When Dylan was old enough he was sent off to Mrs. Hole's School. Walking down three steep blocks in the direction of the port, the little boy came to Mirador Crescent. As he has written,

> never was there such a dame school as ours, so firm and kind and smelling of galoshes, with the sweet and fumbled music of the piano lessons drifting down from the upstairs to the lonely schoolroom, where only the sometimes tearful wicked sat over undone sums, or to repeat a little crime——the pulling of a girl's hair during geography, the sly shin kick under the table during English literature. Behind the school was a narrow lane where only the oldest and boldest threw pebbles at windows, scuffled and boasted, fibbed about their relations . . . and swapped gob-stoppers for slings, old knives for marbles, kite strings for foreign stamps. The lane was always the place to tell your secrets; if you did not have any, you invented them. . . . In the afternoons, when the children were good, they read aloud from Struwelpeter. And when they were bad, they sat alone in the empty classroom, hearing, from above them, the distant, terrible, sad music of the late piano lessons.[1]

The right half of this house is No. 5
Cwmdonkin Drive, Dylan's childhood home

Upper slope of Cwmdonkin Park

The view from Dylan's room

On the way home from Mirador School he would go into the sweet shop of Mrs. Ferguson, who sold the best gob-stoppers and had "pennypackets full of surprises and a sweet kind of glue." Mrs. Ferguson's was the place for the hard-boileds, toffee, fudge, crunches, and marzipan that Dylan continued to love all his life. One of his mates at the school was Mervyn Levy, who has given his own account of one of their adventures:

> My mother died when I was eight and after her death my father engaged a succession of nurses to look after his three children. One of these was a particularly comely and buxom girl whom Dylan and myself had long suspected of washing her breasts in the handbasin. The glass panels of the bathroom door were masked with variously coloured opaque paper, very thin, and imparting to the top half of the door the aspect of a crude, stained-glass window. One day, in the holidays, we carefully scraped away two minute peepholes, one on either side, in readiness for the view that we dreamed would confirm our delicious suspicions. And so, not long afterwards, it turned out. Around three P.M., we crept up the sleepy, dark, afternoon stairs, and with an eye to our respective peepholes, beheld in ecstasy, like two tiny elders, our own Susannah.[2]

At the age of ten, in September, 1925, Dylan went on from the dame school to the Swansea Grammar School, where his father taught English. The memorable event of that first year occurred on the Grammar School sports day in June. The eleven-year-old Dylan entered the mile race, for boys under fifteen, and to everyone's surprise came in first. A picture published in the Cambria Daily Leader the next day shows a thin waif with a limp mop of curls looking too tired to be proud. Twenty-six years later he was still carrying the clipping about with him in his wallet. This was to be one of his few athletic triumphs. Trouble with his lungs began at an early age; catarrh and coughing meant that he had to spend a good deal of his time indoors. Later he attributed a part of his success to this circumstance. "If I'm any good now," he said, "it's because I wasn't allowed to go out to play when it was wet, so I stayed in and read, and got the love of words. There were so many wet days in Swansea when I was a boy." He read, as he put it, "indiscriminately and all the time with my eyes hanging out."

Already he wanted to be a writer, and he first

appeared in print in the Swansea Grammar School Magazine in December, 1925, with a poem whose title, "Song of the Mischievous Dog," anticipated a famous later work. But the ambition to write did not coincide with any disposition to become a scholar. On the contrary; he had already developed the suspicion of everything academic that would last throughout his life. Even in his best subject, English, he suspected the textbook poets. As soon as he had discovered contemporary verse he read it with the enthusiasm of a convert: William Butler Yeats, Richard Aldington, Sacheverell Sitwell, D. H. Lawrence, Gerard Manley Hopkins. While he did not read the schoolbook poets for long, he respected them, and they shared places with the moderns on the wall of his room. There were pictures of Walter de la Mare, Shakespeare, Robert Browning, Stacy Aumonier, Rupert Brooke, and John Greenleaf Whittier, along with his Sunday school certificate and a copy of his own poem "His Requiem," printed in the Western Mail on January 14, 1927.

Life at the Grammar School took on a new dimension when he met the boy who was to be his best friend for the next several years and a good friend all his life. The story of their meeting is described in the chapter of Portrait of the Artist as a Young Dog called "The Fight." Dylan, fourteen, was standing in the schoolyard staring into the yard next door when a strange boy gave him a push. Dylan threw a stone at him and immediately they grappled; Dylan got a black eye and bloodied the older boy's nose. But when a man watching from his garden started encouraging them, they both turned on him, and proceeded to walk away together.

The stranger was Daniel Jenkin Jones, who wore spectacles and announced that he was a composer, and a poet as well: "he had written seven historical novels before he was twelve, and he played the piano and the violin; his mother made wool pictures, his brother was a clerk at the docks and syncopated, his aunt kept a preparatory school on the first floor, and his father wrote music for the organ." They walked on down Gower Road to Sketty, the district just west of the Uplands where Dylan lived, and ended up at Dan's home, Warmley, 38 Eversley Road, a house that was to become their regular rendezvous. Dylan's house had the advantage of being near Cwmdonkin Park and the asthmatic sheep that coughed and the owls that hooted. But Warmley had both a broadcasting station and a cricket pitch. In the back garden of the semidetached house was a stretch twelve feet long where the boys hurled and drove the cricket ball with all their force directly at one another. The Warmley Radio Station has been described, in Dan Jones' words:

THE SONG OF THE MISCHIEVOUS DOG.

There are many who say that a dog has its day,
  And a cat has a number of lives ; '
There are others who think that a lobster is pink,
  And that bees never work in their hives.
There are fewer, of course, who insist that a horse
  Has a horn and two humps on its head.
And a fellow who jests that a mare can build nests
  Is as rare as a donkey that's red.
Yet in spite of all this, I have moments of bliss,
  For I cherish a passion for bones,
And though doubtful of biscuit, I'm willing to risk it,
  And love to chase rabbits and stones.
But my greatest delight is to take a good bite
  At a calf that is plump and delicious ;
And if I indulge in a bite at a bulge,
  Let's hope you won't think me too vicious.

D. M. THOMAS 3A

THE TWO STEINS.

(With apologies to Lewis Carroll).

The Sculptor and the Scientist were walking hand in hand ;
They laughed like anything to see such strife throughout the
  land.
They frolick'd round so merrily, and laughing all the while,
They ran about like lambkins, with a supercilious smile.
They thought it was a mighty joke to see the great upheaval
Which they had brought about to overthrow ideas primeval.
The Sculptor shouted, " People cry aloud for my interment,
Because my Rima in Hyde Park has caused an awful ferment ;
They say that she is quite deformed ; some vandals painted green
My Rima, the epitome of beauty all serene !

Dylan's first published poem

Grammar School Mile Winner.

D. M. Thomas (Mansel), who won the mile race for boys under 15 years of age, at the Swansea Grammar School sports. He is only 12 years of age.

Dylan in September, 1925

Through the W.B.S. system, which consisted of two loud-speakers connected to the pick-up of a radiogram, we were able to broadcast from the upstairs to the downstairs rooms. I still have some of the programmes: "The Rev. Percy will play three piano pieces, Buzzards at Dinner, Salute to Admiral Beattie, and Badgers Beneath My Vest;" "Rebecca Mn will give a recital on the Rebmetpes;" "Locomotive Bowen, the one-eyed cowhand, will give a talk on the Rocking Horse and Varnishing Industry;" "Zoilrebd Pogoho will read his poem Fiffokorp." These broadcasters became real people to us, and we collaborated in a biography of the greatest of them, Percy. Here is a description of one of the trying experiences we inflicted on Percy's old mother: "Near the outskirts of Panama the crippled negress was bitten severely and time upon time, invariably upon the nape, by a white hatshaped bird."[3]

In his 1947 radio broadcast "Return Journey," Dylan had a promenade-man recalling the boy:

About fourteen or fifteen years old . . . with a little red cap. And he used to play by Vivian's Stream. He used to dawdle in the arches . . . and lark about on the railway lines and holler at the old sea. He'd mooch about the dunes and watch the tankers and the tugs and the banana boats come out of the docks. He was going to run away to the sea, he said, I know. On Saturday afternoon he'd go down to the sea when it was a long way out, and hear the foghorns though he couldn't see the ships. And on Sunday nights, after chapel, he'd be swaggering with his pals along the prom, whistling after the girls. [And he tells how a girl would turn to her girl-friend and warn her,] "Don't you say nothing, Hetty, you're only encouraging. No thank you, Mr. Cheeky, with your cut-glass accent and your father's trilby! I don't want no walk on no sands. What d'you say? Ooh, listen to him, Het, he's swallowed a dictionary. No, I don't want to go with nobody up no lane in the moonlight, see, and I'm not a baby-snatcher neither. I seen you going to school along Terrace Road, Mr. Glad-Eye, with your little satchel and wearing your red cap and all."[4]

Dan Jones gives another account of their activities:

> In prose collaboration we had to consult together all the time; the alternate sentence method proved unsuccessful. In poetry collaborations, however, we always wrote alternate lines; I had the odd-numbered lines and Dylan the even-numbered, and we made it a rule that neither of us should suggest an alteration in the other's work. These poems, of which I still have about two hundred, are a different matter from the W.B.S. fooling. It is still play, but it is what I would call serious play. The poetic style of Walter Bram, as we called ourselves, is bafflingly inconsistent; it is fragile, furious, laconic, massive, delicate, incantatory, cool, flinty, violent, Chinese, Greek, and shocking. One poem may begin, "You will be surprised when I remain obdurate," and the next, "I lay under the currant trees and told the beady berries about Jesus." Some of the poems are very, very beautiful; very. Especially those that tell of singularly gentle and godlike action by the third personal plural.

> They had come from the place high on the coral hills
> Where the light from the white sea fills the soil
>   with ascending grace.
> And the sound of their power makes motion as steep
>   as the sky,
> And the fruits of the great ground lie like leaves
>   from a vertical flower.
> They had come from the place; they had come and
>   had gone again
> In a season of delicate rain, in a smooth ascension
>   of grace.[5]

Words were everything—"words occupied Dylan's mind," said Dan Jones, "to the exclusion even of the things with which they have some connection: to him, the cushat and the ring-dove [the same thing] were as different as the ostrich and the humming-bird." Sometimes adjectives took on a comic character quite independent of their meaning so that the innocuous "wilful" or "a certain" could produce a roar of laughter whenever used: "a certain Mrs. Prothero," "a wilful moccasin," or "innumerable bananas." The

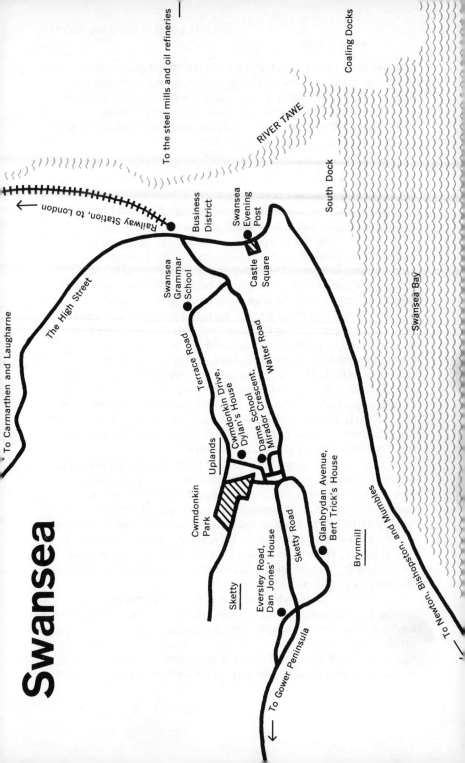

Swansea

To Carmarthen and Laugharne

The High Street

Railway Station, to London

To the steel mills and oil refineries

RIVER TAWE

Coaling Docks

Business District

Swansea Grammar School

Swansea Evening Post

Castle Square

South Dock

Terrace Road

Walter Road

Uplands

Cwmdonkin Drive, Dylan's House

Dame School, Mirador Crescent

Swansea Bay

Cwmdonkin Park

Sketty Road

Glanbrydan Avenue, Bert Trick's House

Brynmill

Sketty

Eversley Road, Dan Jones' House

To Newton, Bishopston, and Mumbles

To Gower Peninsula

boys decided to edit a paper: Dylan to do the literature, Dan to do the music. It was to be called The Thunderer, edited by D. Jenkyn (the name given Dan Jones in "The Fight") and D. Thomas. As Dylan says in the story, "The rhythm was better with D. Thomas and D. Jenkyn, but it was his house." They compromised by planning to write The Thunderer, edited by D. Jenkyn Thomas.

This private publication did not materialize because in July of this same year, 1929, Dylan became joint subeditor of the Swansea Grammar School Magazine. In December he became joint editor, and from December, 1930, through July, 1931, when he left school, he was Editor-in-Chief.

In the Swansea Grammar School, ragging the masters was a familiar sport and plans for upsetting classroom decorum were laid daily. The French master always came to class with a great load of books. One day the boys planted the spindly front legs of his desk so near the edge of the dais that it was barely balanced. When he entered and put his books down, the whole affair crashed to the floor, hitting the front rows of desks, which the boys in turn pushed over. There were screams and pandemonium as the boys pretended to be hit, or to faint, and so succeeded in disrupting work for the day. These high jinks were sometimes aimed at victimizing Dylan. He had always been a rather delicate child, and the bigger bully boys of the class would frequently grab him and stuff him, seat first, into the wastebasket in such a way that he could not get out. It became the regular thing for the master to say as he entered the classroom, "Take Dylan out of the basket."

One master, locked out of his room by the boys, was so afraid of admitting to the principal that he couldn't keep order that there was no class that day. But such shenanigans never took place in the English class conducted by dignified D. J. Thomas. Nobody dared be unruly under his severe gaze. "D. J." was the Senior English Master, much admired for his reading of poetry, particularly that of Edward Thomas. As Ronald Cour, one of Dylan's classmates, said, under D. J.'s tutelage the boys came not so much to love English literature as to admire it.

Despite his rejection of Nonconformist religious dogma, D. J. Thomas was a puritanical man. He had lifted himself from the railwayman's standards of his father to those of the schoolmaster who lived in a semidetached house and had a maid. He had worked hard for his station in life, and it was something of a dismay to discover that his son was not an assiduous student. He had

hoped that Dylan would go on to the university, and perhaps follow
in his own footsteps. The least he expected of Dylan was that he would
be a proper gentleman like himself. But since, as a relative has said,
"No blue-blooded gentleman was a quarter as gentlemanly as Dylan's
father," his hopes were to be denied. His son was, instead, as he
described himself,

> like most boys, no better, brighter, or more
> respectful; he cribbed, mitched, spilt ink, rattled his
> desk and garbled his lessons with the worst of them;
> he could smudge, hedge, smirk, wriggle, wince,
> whimper, blarney, badger, blush, deceive, be
> devious, stammer, improvise, assume offended
> dignity or righteous indignation as though to the
> manner born;
> sullenly and reluctantly he drilled, for some small
> crime, under Sergeant Bird, so wittily nicknamed
> Oiseau, on Wednesday half-holidays, appeared
> regularly in detention classes, hid in the cloakroom
> during algebra, was, when a newcomer, thrown into
> the bushes of the Lower Playground by bigger boys,
> and threw newcomers into the bushes of the Lower
> Playground when he was a bigger boy; he scuffled
> at prayers, he interpolated, smugly, the time-honored
> wrong irreverent words into the morning hymns, he
> helped to damage the headmaster's rhubarb, was
> thirty-third in trigonometry, and, as might be
> expected, edited the School Magazine.[6]

The Reporter

The years between July, 1931, and November, 1934, were in many
ways the most important of Dylan's life. It was during this time that he
held his first job, gained experience as an actor, fell in love, had his
first sexual experience, and wrote the poetry and prose that were
to make up much of his first three books. He had left school in July,
1931 (without taking any of the examinations but the one in
English), and, in the depths of the Depression, had the good luck to
find a job as a proofreader and, after several months, as an apprentice
reporter on the South Wales Daily Post; his first article was entitled
"Nellie Wallace's Mimicry."

Wynford Vaughan Thomas went with the cub reporter
when he made his call on the famous music-hall performer backstage

Dylan and his mother

The newspaper office

Article from the <u>Herald of Wales</u>

at the Swansea Empire Theatre. Dylan had asked his friend if he
would care to meet an actress, and the invitation was made to sound as
if the entire glamorous backstage world was to be spread out before
them. They arrived outside her dressing room, held their breath, and
knocked. The beloved Nellie Wallace—who must have been more
than sixty-five—called out in a cracked voice, "Come in, dearie."

Dylan, straightening up his frail five and a half feet,
announced, "Miss Wallace, we bring you the homage of the artists
of the future for the artists of the past." Miss Wallace asked if they
were variety or legit. Legit, they replied, not knowing one from the
other. "In that case, boys, you've got a hell of a road to travel! Have
some gin?" When they took the drink, it exploded in their mouths.
Watching them, Miss Wallace chortled and said that at least this was
one case where the artists of the past could wipe the floor with
the artists of the future. And she downed her gin with a quick and
practiced gulp. She gave a finishing touch to her preposterous hunting
costume, put a feather in her pile of red hair, and went prancing
out onto the stage singing about the gallant hunter—"I was after the
fox, me boys, but he was after me." Dylan said to his friend that
they must never tell anyone—they must keep it for their memoirs.

As an apprentice on the Post and the associated
weekly Herald of Wales, Dylan traveled about with a senior reporter to
learn the ropes. Soon he was being given routine assignments of his
own: reporting soccer matches, reviewing plays, and the like. A typical
day is recorded in his notebook: "Called at British Legion. Nothing.
Called at Hospital. One broken leg. Auction at the Metropole. Ring
Mr. Beyon re Gymanfa Ganu. Lunch. Pint and pasty at the Singleton
with Mrs. Giles. Bazaar at Bethesda Chapel. Chimney on fire at
Tontine Street. Walters Road Sunday School Outing. Rehearsal of the
Mikado at Skewen—all front page stuff." It may not have been
front-page stuff, but local reporting was important to the editor. Dylan
did not endear himself to his boss when, on a crucial occasion, he
skipped visiting the hospital and thereby failed to report the sudden
death of the matron. He preferred to spend his time playing billiards at
the YMCA, or to drop in at the Three Lamps or some other pub to have
a pint with one of his colleagues—Fred Farr, Half Hook, Bill Latham,
Cliff Williams, Gareth Hughes, Eric Hughes, or Glyn Lowery. One
of these pub-crawling evenings with Fred Farr provided the material
for the story in Portrait of the Artist as a Young Dog entitled
"Old Garbo."

Early in his career as a cub reporter, Dylan was
invited by Farr to join him for a drink one evening. Farr, enviable in

Dylan, c. 1938

Dylan's eyes as a great shorthand writer, was "a chain-smoker, a bitter drinker, very humorous, round-faced and round-bellied, with dart holes in his nose." Once upon a time he might have been "a mincing-mannered man, with a strut and a cane to balance it, a watch-chain across the waistcoat, a gold tooth, even, perhaps a flower from his own garden in his buttonhole. But now each attempt at a precise gesture was caked and soaked before it began; when he placed the tips of his thumb and forefinger together, you saw only the cracked nails in mourning and the Woodbine stains." (It was in imitation of Fred Farr that Dylan adopted the practice of dangling his cigarette from his lower lip.) They were to meet in the back bar of The Three Lamps. Dylan arrived early and ordered a pint: "I leant against the bar, between an alderman and a solicitor, drinking bitter, wishing that my father could see me now and glad, at the same time, that he was visiting Uncle A. in Aberavon. He could not fail to see that I was a boy no longer, nor fail to be angry at the angle of my fag and my hat and the threat of the clutched tankard. I liked the taste of beer, its live, white lather, its brass-bright depths, the sudden world through the wet-brown walls of the glass, the tilted rush to the lips and the slow swallowing down to the lapping belly, the salt on the tongue, the foam at the corners." Farr arrived; they finished their drinks and moved on to the bar of the Carlton Hotel. There miners, singing around the piano, their faces pocked, their broad hands scarred and damaged, made jokes with the barmaid. "Oh! to be able to join in the suggestive play or the rocking choir . . . or to be called 'saucy' and 'a one' as I joked and ogled at the counter, making innocent, dirty love that would come to nothing among the spilt beer and piling glasses." They moved on to a third pub, the Fishguard, down by the rocks, where they expected to see the knitting sailors; there Dylan had his first glass of rum. But suddenly "two small men, Mr. Farr and his twin brother, led me on an ice-rink to the door, and the night air slapped me down." The wall came up to him and knocked off his new soft felt trilby. When he came around again, he was in the Lord Jersey. There they met up with another reporter, Ted Williams, and the barmaid gave Dylan a glad eye. "A broken baritone voice spoiled the chorus; I recognized it as my own, and drowned it." They returned for a nightcap to the Fishguard and "the bench spun. The cabin of the Fishguard tilted." The boy had had enough. "The last tram clanked home. I did not have the penny for the fare. 'You get off here. Careful!' The revolving hill to my father's house reached to the sky. Nobody was up. I crept to a wild bed, and the wallpaper lakes converged and sucked me down."

    He has described himself as he looked then—"above medium height. Above medium height for Wales, I mean, he's five foot six and a half. Thick blubber lips; snub nose; curly mouse-brown hair; one front tooth broken after playing a game called cats and dogs in the Mermaid, Mumbles; speaks rather fancy, truculent; plausible; a bit of a shower-off; plus fours and no breakfast, you know . . . a bombastic adolescent provincial bohemian with a thick-knotted artist's tie made out of his sister's scarf—she never knew where it had gone—and a cricket-shirt dyed bottle green; a gabbing, ambitious, mock-tough, pretentious young man; and mole-y, too."[7] That he was not so tough was clear when an old reporter took him to the morgue—"you got to be <u>persona grata</u> in the mortuary, see." When they arrived, workmen, whom Dylan didn't notice, were adding a new coat of paint to the ceiling. His eyes were fixed on a slab when one of the painters high up on a ladder boomed out, "Good morning, gents." Dylan, already pale green, turned white and fled.

    Although certain feature stories such as "Genius and Madness Akin in the World of Art" were signed, most of Dylan's contributions to the <u>Swansea Post</u> were anonymous. In the weekly <u>Herald of Wales</u>, however, he had his own byline. That he was the periodical's authority on poetry is clear from the titles: "The Poets of Swansea: Walter Savage Landor to James Chapman Woods," "Tragedy of Swansea's Comic Genius," "The Story of Llewelyn Prichard, Author of Twm Shon Catti"; two articles, "Minor Poets of Old Swansea," "Verse of James Chapman Woods, a Critical Estimate, Swansea's Greatest Poet"; and "A Modern Poet of Gower: Mr. E. Howard Harris." An exception to his pieces on poetry was a feature article about his Uncle Dai's church, "The Story of Paraclete." Three of his poems also appeared in the <u>Herald</u>: "Youth Calls to Age" (April 23, 1932), "Greek Play in a Garden" (July 15, 1933), and "Poet, 1935" (June 8, 1935).

    While Dylan worked as a cub on the paper, he planned to continue his school career as editor. In the June 2, 1931, <u>South Wales Post</u> the following announcement appeared:

> Some time ago it was announced in this column
> that Swansea might shortly expect a new literary
> publication, entitled <u>Prose and Verse</u>. It is, as was
> then mentioned, to be published by subscription,
> and although the editor hopes to be able to reduce
> the price of subsequent issues, the price of the
> first copy is to be two shillings. It is necessary to sell

at least two hundred copies at this price in order
to cover the initial expenses. The editor, who is to be
found at 5 Cwmdonkin Drive, Uplands, wants
contributions, and he says that "their only
qualification must be originality of outlook and
expression."[8]

Two years later, in October of 1933, Dylan wrote to Trevor Hughes,
one of those who had responded to the original invitation:

Prose and Verse, that stillborn child, is to be
resurrected. Grocer Trick is to do the financial and
business part of it, and I, as it was arranged before,
am to edit it. The high standards formerly set
will be strictly adhered to, but there is one
important new condition. "P & V" will print only the
work of Welshmen and women and this includes
those of dim Welsh ancestry and those born in Wales
—who write in English. This condition necessarily
restricts, but it is that which will make, I hope and
trust, the journal an unique affair. Another highbrow
periodical, especially produced from a blowsy town
such as this—on the furthest peaks of the literary
world—is damned to hell from the beginning. But
a new high-class periodical for Welshmen?
Up Cymru! I don't see why it shouldn't be a great
success.[9]

But again the idea was stillborn. Ultimately another Welshman,
Keidrych Rhys, had a similar idea and launched the
distinguished and successful Wales. One of Dylan's stories,
"Prologue to an Adventure," was featured on the front cover of
Volume 1, Number 1 (Summer, 1937), and his poems and stories
appeared in many of the succeeding issues.

Dylan had been hired for a trial year as an
apprentice reporter. At the end of the year he was discharged because
he couldn't or wouldn't master shorthand—at least that was the
official reason. But it was obvious from the beginning that he had
neither the temperament nor the interest to make reporting a
profession. To record factual happenings was not his talent. During
these months, when he should have been attending to church bazaars,
auctions, broken legs, soccer games, and Sunday school outings, he
was storing up the experience that was to give substance to the
Portrait of the Artist as a Young Dog. And he was actually writing such

Fountain in the Park

Cwmdonkin Park bandstand

poems as "Today, This Insect, and the World I Breathe," "The Spire Cranes," "Why East Wind Chills," "Out of the Sighs" and "The Hunchback." Ideas for poems would come during strolls through his childhood world, Cwmdonkin Park, where he would see familiar figures—the boys, Smoky the park keeper, and the hunchback who slept in a kennel.

The Hunchback in the Park

The hunchback in the park
A solitary mister
Propped between trees and water
From the opening of the garden lock
That lets the trees and water enter
Until the Sunday sombre bell at dark

Eating bread from a newspaper
Drinking water from the chained cup
That the children filled with gravel
In the fountain basin where I sailed my ship
Slept at night in a dog kennel
But nobody chained him up.

Like the park birds he came early
Like the water he sat down
And Mister they called Hey mister
The truant boys from the town
Running when he had heard them clearly
On out of sound

Past lake and rockery
Laughing when he shook his paper
Hunchbacked in mockery
Through the loud zoo of the willow groves
Dodging the park keeper
With his stick that picked up leaves.

And the old dog sleeper
Alone between nurses and swans
While the boys among willows
Made the tigers jump out of their eyes
To roar on the rockery stones
And the groves were blue with sailors

Made all day until bell time
A woman figure without fault
Straight as a young elm
Straight and tall from his crooked bones
That she might stand in the night
After the locks and chains

All night in the unmade park
After the railings and shrubberies
The birds the grass the trees the lake
And the wild boys innocent as strawberries
Had followed the hunchback
To his kennel in the dark.

The Young Poet

From the day he left grammar school to the day he went to London, Dylan experienced one of the most prolific bursts of poetic creativity he was ever to enjoy. Between April, 1930, and April, 1934 (between the ages of sixteen and nineteen), he produced well over 212 poems—averaging more than one a week in a four-year period of continuous production. Not by any means apprentice work, these included the first versions of some of his greatest poems— "The Hunchback in the Park," "After the Funeral," "The Force that Through the Green Fuse," and "I See the Boys of Summer." When he was eighteen and nineteen he composed all of his first book, 18 Poems, and nearly half of the poems which were later to appear in Twenty-Five Poems (1936) and The Map of Love (1939).

His appearance in print outside the pages of the school magazine had begun with "His Requiem," published in the Western Mail when he was twelve. In the same year, the Boy's Own Paper had published a poem. But these were strictly juvenilia. His first appearance in a national magazine came about through his acquaintance with Albert E. Trick.

Trick ran a small grocery store at 69 Glanbrydan Avenue, just a few blocks down the hill from Dylan's house. He was in his early thirties, and had published poems and articles in the Swansea Guardian, the Western Counties Gazette, and the Christian Agitator. An active Socialist, he was a member of the Executive Committee of the Swansea Labour Party, the editor of their monthly journal New Outlook, and editor of a local weekly run by the unemployed.

One evening in the winter of 1931–1932, Bert Trick

Dylan

answered his door to discover a young-looking seventeen-year-old boy with a mop of curly hair, round wondering eyes and pouty lips, holding a pork-pie hat, and trying, Trick thought, to look very sophisticated. Thomas Taig, who ran the Little Theatre and was an English lecturer at University College, Swansea, had recommended that Dylan bring his poems for Trick's opinion. The boy was invited to come back the following evening at seven, and thus began a friendship that became very close for the next few years. Bert Trick, in an interview, recalled their first meeting:

> I invited him into my sitting room and we sat and discussed all sorts of things, sizing each other up, and after an hour or so, I asked, "Would you like now that I read your poems?" And he said, "Oh, no, poems shouldn't be read; they should be spoken." Whereupon, he pulled a rolled-up blue school exercise book out of his pocket, sat back in the easy chair, with his leg over one arm, and in an arresting voice started to read some of his early poems. I was astonished. It was clear that here was a poet singing in a new voice. After he had read three poems and he had asked me what I thought of them, we discussed them. I was so impressed that I wanted Nell, my wife, to meet him so I went in the next room on grounds of fetching coffee and told Nell, "I've found a genius. You must come and hear this." And she, too, immediately fell under the spell of the words and the voice.[10]

This was the first of what later became regular twice-a-week meetings with Trick and a group of their mutual friends. On Wednesday nights it was at 5 Cwmdonkin Drive; there Dylan would read his work in progress, read and discuss poetry, and entertain the guests. On Sunday nights a similar group met at the Tricks'. The nucleus of the Sunday group consisted of Dylan, Nell and Bert Trick, Fred Janes the painter, and Tom Warner the composer. A larger circle developed around the original one and often numbered twelve or fourteen people. Dylan, with his theatrical flair, could evoke tears when he was in one of his anecdotal moods, accurately mimicking any dialect. But he disliked anything to be stage-managed. If anyone tried to make him show off, he immediately became the diffident, awkward, what-do-you-mean? boy.

> I remember [wrote Bert Trick] one occasion at those Sunday evening meetings that we had; a friend

of mine who happened to be a labor councillor,
knowing that I was friendly with Dylan, asked if it
was possible for his wife to meet him. She would very
much like to meet this up-and-coming young poet:
she had pretensions to some culture. Well, I said,
you're very welcome to come to our house on Sunday
evening. It's a regular meeting at my place, and
there may be a dozen people turn up. Dylan will be
there, and if you care to bring your wife along, we
would be very happy to welcome the both of you.
I made the mistake on Wednesday evening of telling
Dylan that I'd invited these people to meet him. On
the Sunday, everybody came—but Dylan. No
explanation, he just wasn't there. The evening went
on more or less as usual, but it wasn't lit up with the
fantastic wit and nonsense of Dylan which made an
evening a memorable occasion, and our guests
parted about midnight. I was helping Nell to clear up
after the visitors, when there was a very timid knock
on the back door. Nell went, and standing there,
looking very contrite, full of apologies was Dylan.
I couldn't face it, he said. Come in, Dylan. Dylan sat
down then, and he had a special supper all his own.
And then we returned to our sitting room and we
sat and talked and had the usual Dylan evening
until about three o'clock in the morning.[11]

One of the places in which Dylan liked to write poems was the
village of Rhossilli at the furthest point of Gower, a place of
wild, bleak beauty. He would often go down in the mornings with a
book and a bag of food and stay there until evening. On one day
of dreadful memory he walked out, at low tide, over the reef, onto
the massive Worm of rock that juts into the channel. He said that the
gulls and rats there were the millionth generation of the winged
and tailed families that screamed in the air and ran through
the grass when the first sea scudded on Rhossilli beach. There is
one stretch of rock covered with long yellow grass—walking on it
one felt like something out of the "Tales of Mystery and
Imagination," treading for an eternity, on the long hairs of
rats. He had gone out on the Worm in the early afternoon and, going
to the very end, had fallen asleep in the sun, even though the gulls
were screaming wildly. When he awoke the sun was rapidly going
down. He ran over the rocks, over the abominable grass, to the reef

The Worm's Head, Gower Peninsula

Bert and Nell Trick at Caswell Bay, Gower

—but the tide had come in. He had to sit there, surrounded by the creatures of the dark, for hours. Not till midnight did the tips of the reef begin to appear and only then was he able to climb over them to the shore. On the eighteen-mile walk home in the dark he saw everything from snails, lizards, glowworms, and hares to diaphanous young ladies in white who vanished as he approached.

In the summertime Dylan would often join Bert and Nell Trick and their young daughter Pamela for week-ends at their summer bungalow on Gower's Caswell Bay. Dylan loved to walk and he and Trick hiked for miles along the shore. At the house they would play a sort of two-man cricket match in which Dylan showed himself an extremely good, fast bowler. In the evenings, after the usual brilliant sunsets over the bay, there would be sessions around the Dover stove. By the light of a paraffin lamp Dylan would pull out his current blue exercise book and read aloud the poems he was working on, or some of the stories about the people of the Jarvis Valley. It was here he first read the sketch that was to evolve into Under Milk Wood, at that time a short piece about events in a row of terrace houses in a typical Welsh seaside town called Llareggub. Bert Trick, on hearing the name, said, "Well, Dylan, that's the first time I've ever heard you use a Welsh word in anything you've written." Dylan gave a rather naughty look and said, "Bert, it's an anagram: just read it backwards."

The Actor

One of Dylan's best friends during his year on the Post was a fellow reporter, Eric Hughes, with whom he spent a good deal of time in activities connected with the little theatre group in Mumbles. A Stage Society formed in 1929 had taken over a church-school hall at Southend, Mumbles, and there performed Capek, Barrie, Galsworthy, Housman, and Shaw. It was an active group that included young people as well as businessmen and their wives. Whole families worked on sets and costumes, played in the orchestra, and took roles. The first production in which Hughes and Thomas appeared was Noel Coward's Hay Fever. Both boys were praised for their acting, as were Dylan's sister Nancy and the man she was shortly to marry, Haydn Taylor.

Dylan's career as a man of the theatre had actually begun back in grammar school days when, fourteen years old, he played Edward Stanton in John Drinkwater's Abraham Lincoln. In a 1929 issue of the Grammar School Magazine appeared his skit

"Desert Idyll" satirizing the orotund solemnity of the British play
of the East and the antics of pseudo-sheiks like Rudolph Valentino:
Ben el Rhubarb's beautiful daughter spurned the Jub of Tony-Pandy
for her handsome lover, Horace el Tureen, and a chorus heightened
the dramatic moments with suitably pitched wails.

In the spring of 1930 Dylan was chosen for the
lead in Oliver Cromwell. With heavy make-up he tried to impersonate
the aging Cromwell but, a reviewer said, "he looked as young and
as fresh and clean as if he had just come off the cover of a chocolate
box." Undaunted, he proceeded in the following year to take on the
role of the tough labor leader in the school production of Galsworthy's
Strife. The school paper reported "There were times when [D. M.
Thomas] seemed to lack the coarseness and toughness of fibre
necessary for the interpretation of Roberts; his vowels were
occasionally too genteel and he was innocent of gesture, an essential
part of the demagogue's equipment. Still, Thomas is too good an
actor to make a hash of any part, and he successfully survived an
ordeal that would make heavy demands upon a mature and
experienced actor."[12]

The plays were put on in the YMCA's Llewelyn Hall;
both tense and tender scenes were likely to be punctuated by
rhythmic thuds from the gymnasium above. Dylan was not only a
school actor but a promoter as well: he helped found a reading circle
of some twenty-five members whose opening project was Galsworthy's
Escape. In the debating society he established, the founder and his
colleague lost the motion "That Modern Youth is Decadent" despite
Dylan's speaking "with Cymric fire."

Dylan wrote revue sketches for the Little Theatre,
took on jobs as an extra in the local YMCA Players, and came into his
own with the Mumbles Stage Society. After Hay Fever, he played
Count Bellair in Farquhar's The Beaux' Stratagem and, as his
colleague Ethel Ross reported, remedied for all time the fault of
being "innocent of gesture." His next play, H. F. Rubinstein's Peter
and Paul, had a kind of oblique relevance to his own later life.
J. D. Williams, editor of the South Wales Evening Post, described it:

> Peter [Dylan], determined to write, has to buckle
> to and carry on his father's business, and in that
> atmosphere he forgets how to write and does a
> nobler thing: he rears a happy family. But Peter, in
> age reviewing his life, feels that he has missed its
> biggest meaning: the unwritten books haunt him.
>
> Paul [Eric Hughes], who longed for the bourgeois

> comforts of a home, is deflected on to the path of
> the writer, and suffers long neglect and persecution
> and the breaking-up of his home before the people
> acclaim his fame.[13]

The next play, Rodney Ackland's Strange Orchestra, also had certain
relevant overtones, as Williams described it:

> The Little Theatre players, or perhaps mainly the
> younger spirits among them, gave us the racking
> disharmonies, individual and communal,
> concentrated in one household.
>
> Near the end, when the play was deeply stirring,
> there are hints of approaching serenity for a few,
> achieved through suffering, but even so, it can hardly
> be complained that there are left any allurements
> in the "life" of these temperamental folk with their
> incessant introspection and selfishness, their swift
> "loves," their fun parties and clubs and their gin
> and sandwiches.
>
> The lodgers include an amoral cad: a young
> novelist, Val, so absorbed in himself, in dramatising
> his friends for his novels that he cannot see the
> greatness of Esther's piteous realisation of life's
> cruelties. There was a pitiable inevitability about
> Mr. Dylan Thomas's Val.[14]

Dylan's last important role was Witwoud in Congreve's
The Way of the World in which his elegance of movement and
mastery of gesture were praised. While preparing for another
large part, immediately afterward, he got into trouble. During
rehearsals those actors who were not actually in the current scene
had a habit of spending their waiting time in the bar of a hotel called
Cheese's in Mumbles. Some of the young men and the more daring
of the girls were often provokingly missing when they were needed,
and had to be sent for by special messenger. The producer of this
play, Doreen Goodridge, had been often enough annoyed by this
difficulty to warn Thomas in particular that if he went to the hotel he
needn't come back. When on the day before the opening he did
just that, he was peremptorily dismissed. The play went on with the
understudy and Dylan's relations with the group were never again the
same. He did later take a minor part in Richard II, in April, 1934,
and in a charity revival of Hay Fever, but by this time his more
important role as a writer was developing, and his eyes were turning
toward London.

The Prize Winner

Throughout the first year of their frequent meetings, Bert Trick had urged Dylan to submit his work to a national publication. Dylan answered his suggestion with an interested look but no action. While not shy about proclaiming his verses on Glanbrydan Avenue or Cwmdonkin Drive, Dylan seemed not to want to enter into competition with the newly famous poets of the day: W. H. Auden, Stephen Spender, Cecil Day Lewis, Louis MacNeice. The trend of the times was toward social analysis and political action and away from the fury of personal lyricism which Dylan offered. Auden was writing, in "A Bride in the 30's,"

> Ten million of the desperate marching by,
> Five feet, six feet, seven feet high,
> Hitler and Mussolini in their wooing poses,
> Churchill acknowledging the voters' greeting,
> Roosevelt at the microphone. . . .

There seemed no place for a word-obsessed romantic.

But Trick persisted and, after much persuasion, got Dylan to send two poems off to A. R. Orage, editor of the New English Weekly, who had been the discoverer of a number of young writers. A week or so after he had sent the poems off, Dylan came round to Trick's with a crumpled letter among a lot of other crumpled papers in his pocket. "I had a letter from Orage," he said. "Would you like to read it, Bert?" It turned out to be a piece of extravagant praise for the poems that Dylan had sent, urging him to send more. "But look, he hasn't paid me for them!" "Oh," said Trick, "they don't pay for contributions, the New English Weekly. The fact that you have been published there means that already you have a kind of reputation as a poet." "Oh, damn that, I can't buy Woodbines or beers on that. I'm not sending him any more." However, he did send more. The paper published "And Death Shall Have No Dominion" (May 18, 1933), "Out of the Pit" (January 25, 1934), and the stories "After the Fair" (March 15, 1934) and "The End of the River" (November 22, 1934). Later, when Dylan had established his name with the publication of 18 Poems, he was to become a frequent contributor to the New English Weekly: poems in three issues in the summer of 1936; the story "A Visit to Grandpa's" (March, 1938); and reviews of recent fiction in seven issues of 1938 and in three issues of 1939.

In the meantime Dylan had discovered a better place

to send his poems. Hayter Preston, literary editor of the London
<u>Sunday Referee</u>, had allotted a poetry half-column to Victor
Benjamin Neuburg which very quickly grew to a full column. The
"Poets' Corner" offered a weekly prize of half a guinea to the major
prize poem, and there were minor prizes and honorable mentions
as well. Already the discerning Neuburg and his assistant Sheila
MacLeod had discovered such writers as Pamela Hansford Johnson
and David Gascoyne. The competition had been going about four
months when Dylan sent in his first entry, "That Sanity Be Kept." It
became a major prize winner and was printed on September 3, 1933.
After that Dylan regularly sent in poems and, though not every one
was printed, of those that were, none failed to get a prize or a
mention. His second major prize poem was printed on October 29,
two days after his nineteenth birthday: "The Force that Through the
Green Fuse Drives the Flower." Here appeared those parallel themes
of vitality and mortality that were to continue throughout all his
poems and stories:

The Force that through the Green Fuse Drives the Flower

The force that through the green fuse drives the flower
Drives my green age; that blasts the roots of trees
Is my destroyer.
And I am dumb to tell the crooked rose
My youth is bent by the same wintry fever.

The force that drives the water through the rocks
Drives my red blood; that drives the mouthing streams
Turns mine to wax.
And I am dumb to mouth unto my veins
How at the mountain spring the same mouth sucks.

The hand that whirls the water in the pool
Stirs the quicksand; that ropes the blowing wind
Hauls my shroud sail.
And I am dumb to tell the hanging man
How of my clay is made the hangman's lime.

The lips of time leech to the fountain head;
Love drips and gathers, but the fallen blood
Shall calm her sores.
And I am dumb to tell a weather's wind
How time has ticked a heaven round the stars.

> And I am dumb to tell the lover's tomb
> How at my sheet goes the same crooked worm.

Pamela Hansford Johnson

Five more poems were to be printed in the <u>Sunday Referee</u>, the last appearing in August, 1935. The particular poem which had first attracted the attention of Victor Neuburg was a twenty-three-line poem which rather obviously echoed T. S. Eliot; it began

> That sanity be kept I sit at open windows,
> Regard the sky, make unobtrusive comment on the
>   moon,
> Sit at open windows in my shirt,
> And let the traffic pass, the signals shine,
> The engines run, the brass bands keep in tune,
> For sanity must be preserved.

Shortly afterward he wrote that the more he thought about the poem the less he liked it. The idea of himself sitting in his shirtsleeves in the open window imagining himself as some Jehovah of the West was, he thought, rather odd. If he were an Apollo, it would have been different, but in fact he was a little person with much untidy hair. The person to whom he wrote this was Pamela Hansford Johnson, who had been pleased by the poem and had written the unknown author to tell him so. Thus began in September, 1933, a correspondence which was gradually to increase in frequency until the two met the following February. Early on, Dylan explained that his name, rhyming with "chillun," came "for some mad reason" from the <u>Mabinogion</u> and means the "Prince of Darkness." (In fact, the name Dylan in the Welsh epic is called "the son of the Wave.") He described himself as about five foot six, weighing about 122 pounds, with rat-coloured brown hair, big eyes mixed brown and green, three moles on the right cheek, feet size five, and a baritone voice——though sometimes it swept toward tenor and sometimes drooped towards bass.

He said that his schoolmaster father was much more broadminded than his mother who came from the farmlands of Carmarthensire. His only sister Nancy had passed through the phases of schoolgirl, flapper, and social snob into a comfortable marriage. He had first met tobacco, the Boy Scout's Enemy, and poetry, the Spinster's Friend, when he was in dame school. Alcohol, the Demon

Twenty Three.

The force that through the green fuse drives the flower
Drives my green age; that blasts the roots of trees
Is my destroyer.
~~And~~ I am dumb to tell the ~~eaten~~ rose
How at my sheet goes the same crooked worm,
And dumb to holla thunder to the skies
How at my cloths flies the same central
~~storm~~

The force that through the green fuse drives the flower
Drives my green age; that blasts the roots of trees
Is my destroyer.
And I am dumb to tell the crooked rose
My youth is bent by the same wintry fever.

The force that drives the water through the rocks
Drives my red blood; that dries the mouthing
                                              streams
Turns mine to wax.

King, he met when a senior at the Grammar School. Having spent a term on a paper reporting news of Calvinistic chapels and mortuaries, he said, he was now doing nothing but writing and earning a few guineas by his acting.

They exchanged photographs and when Pamela's arrived he found her appearance formidable and called her Wilhelmina. He did not expect her to be so full and bright and strong, with such a British chin, and with such a dominant personality. And he defined his own small chinless self as an emasculate Eton boy in comparison. Very quickly they began exchanging and criticizing each other's poetry. Dylan always professed to admire her verse, but his comments were scathing. It was, he finally got around to saying, sweet, girlish drivel. Her poetry, he told her, was born out of Christina Rossetti and the Georgian and Poetry Bookshop gang. He was going to knock the romanticist warbling out of her head. And there were long discussions about subject matter, simplicity versus obscurity, and vocabulary: For each word like jasmine that she was prepared to give up, he offered to surrender a word like belly. But he refused to give up any of his "wormy wombs." He said they were two extremists: one upstairs in our lady's chamber and the other downstairs in our lady's chamberpot. Still, he said, he would try to comb the superfluous horrors out of his beard if she would promise to let spring pass next year without bestowing a single lavish spate on its tomb.

He professed a theoretical admiration for Byron, Keats, and Shelley, but he had harsh things to say of Wordsworth, who was a tea-time bore, the great frost of literature, the verbose, the humourless, the platitudinary reporter of Nature in her dullest of moods. He said he, himself, was on the path of Blake, but so far behind him that only the wings of his heels were in sight. He used to read her poems as well as his own (and passages from Macbeth, Beddoes' Death's Jest Book, and Blake's Prophetic Books) out loud, chanting them in a booming voice so that the neighbors must have known them all by heart. He said that he thought that baths were built especially for poets to lie in to intone aloud amid the steam and boiling ripples.

He has described the two libraries in his house—his father's and his. His Dad's room was full of all the accepted things from Chaucer to Henry James, all the encyclopedias and books of reference, all Saintsbury, and innumerable books on the theory of literature. His library contained nearly everything that a respectable highbrow library should contain. Dylan's books, on the other hand, were nearly all poetry, and mostly modern. He had the collected poems of Manley Hopkins, Stephen Crane, Yeats, de la Mare, Osbert Sitwell, Wilfred Owen, W. H. Auden, and T. S. Eliot; volumes of poetry by Aldous Huxley, Sacheverell and Edith Sitwell, Edna St. Vincent Millay, D. H. Lawrence, Humbert Wolfe, Siegfried Sassoon, and Harold Monro; most of the Best Poems of the Year; two of the Georgian anthologies, one of the Imagist anthologies; Whips and Scorpions (modern satiric verse), the London Mercury anthology, the Nineties Anthology; a volume of Cambridge poetry and Oxford undergraduate poetry; most of Lawrence, most of Joyce with the exception of Ulysses, all Gilbert Murray's Greek translations, some Shaw, a little Virginia Woolf, and some E. M. Forster.

He told her about his career as an actor, how he traveled about as Witwoud in The Way of the World playing in Welsh-speaking valleys where they didn't understand one bawdy word from the beginning to the end. He explained that his specialty was playing madmen, neurotics, nasty modern young men, and low comedians. When he learned that Pamela acted too, he suggested that if she played hysterical young women with tumors or erotic young things with Notions the two should join up and play Grand Guignol in the provincial music halls. This talk finally led to Dylan's writing a long letter in the form of a one-act play with the title "Spajma and Salnady or Who Shot the Emu?" the names of the two principals, Spajma Oh-no-nel and Salnady Moth, being anagrams on both their names. The scene was set in a large red-and-puce-curtained hall: Scarlet bananas were painted on the ceiling and the skins of dead lepers covered the floor; there were knobs on nearly everything— except on the doors. In the corners of the room were garrotted ancient herbalists along with the left arms of a few postmen and the complete works of John Galsworthy. The curtain rises on total darkness which is undisturbed for three hours. At last a tiny voice is heard asking Albert for Christ's sake to put on the light; whereupon the audience sees revealed The Spirit of Poetry—a fat lady in a fireman's costume. Salnady and Spajma proceed to debate with the Spirit and to exchange opinions with each other. Dylan-Salnady announces that the films he has enjoyed include "The Cabinet of Dr. Caligari," "Atalanta," "Student of Prague," "Edge of the World," "Vaudeville," "Waxworks," "The Street," "M," "The Blue Angel," "Sous les Toits de Paris," "Potemkin," "The Gold Rush," "The Three Little Pigs," and the Marx Brothers comedies. After an extended and spirited exchange in which Salnady denounces the title of Pamela-Spajma's forthcoming book of poems (Symphony for Full

Orchestra), the two climb up a series of talking mountains and no one knows what is going to happen next as the curtain falls.

Dylan's way of composing his letters to Pamela was generally to jot down random ideas on scraps of paper. After accumulating a sufficient quantity, he would copy them out in ink, giving each a little headline in the margin, onto large sheets, and then mail off from five to twelve pages at a time. In one of them he described a typical day in the fall of 1933. He would wake up to find an apple, a banana, and a cigarette beside his bed for breakfast. He would have these in bed with the morning Telegraph. Then he would shave, smoking a second cigarette. Then the morning would be spent reading whatever was at hand, poetry or prose, translations from the Greek, the Film Pictorial, a new novel from Smith's lending library, a new book of criticism, or an old favorite like Grimm or George Herbert. Around noon he would wander down the hill to the Uplands Hotel for a pint or two of beer before returning home for lunch and reading in front of the fire. The afternoon would be filled with writing a poem, a story, or a letter, or taking his devils for an airing—a lonely walk over the desolate Gower cliffs. After tea he would read or write again until six, and then to Mumbles to a pub or two—the Marine, the Antelope, or the Mermaid. There would likely be an eight o'clock rehearsal at the Little Theatre; otherwise the evening would be spent in talk at a pub, a three-mile walk home to supper, more reading and writing. It wasn't a very British day, according to him, with its excessive thinking, talking, and alcohol.

As the correspondence with Pamela continued with increasing frequency and intimacy, a note of flirtation crept in. He told her that there was an imp in her room looking with his eyes at her. In one letter he went into a long discourse on the inhumanity of society's attitudes towards sex in adolescence. He pointed out that our laws were medieval when they forced virginity upon young people at that time of their lives when they most needed sexual expression. Our society, he asserted, looks upon sexual relations as not only unnecessary but unclean. The physical expression of sex must be repressed until a marriage is economically feasible. And then, after enough, the opportunity comes only when love has turned to lust and sadism, and the mind is soured by inhibitions. Dylan's suggestion was that from the first months of puberty, the sexual activities of boys and girls should be encouraged. The family of a girl to whom a boy had been attracted should open their house to the boy, and vice versa. He felt that their sleeping together would keep both brains and bodies perpetually clean and that they would both grow up physically and mentally uncontaminated. Dylan was aware that in his program he was attacking the very foundations of his corrupted hemisphere, but he saw no wrong in this. Each boy and girl was to have as many lovers as he wished—there would be no binding agreements—until finally each would find the lover with whom he wanted to live for a longer time, or for ever.

Pamela, a _jeune fille bien élevée_, was not quite equal to this daring, for which Dylan chided her. She had written him that, after all, a person really knew what sex meant even before he had experienced it. Dylan snorted back that such an extraordinary statement would require a good deal of explaining away at the gates of heaven where the phallus was taken as a fact rather than as a peg on which to hang platitudes.

By now Dylan wanted to meet his correspondent, and began to make plans to go to the city. His sister Nancy had recently married and moved to London, and he decided he might visit her and at the same time set about looking for a job. Nancy Thomas, born September 2, 1906, had often taken a nursemaid's care of her eight-year-younger brother. In May, 1933, she had married her fellow actor Haydn Taylor, an industrial surveyor, and they had moved to a houseboat at Henley-on-Thames. Later she was to join the Women's Territorial Army, the section called FANY (Female, Auxiliary Nursing Yeomanry), as a driver for officers. Around 1943 she was drafted to India and there divorced Taylor to become the wife of a Colonel Summersbee who was in private life an accountant; she remained in India until she died of cancer at the age of forty-seven in the same year as Dylan, 1953. According to a long-time friend, she was a gay, versatile, witty person, fond of amateur acting and was an avid sailor. She was affectionate toward Dylan and inordinately proud of Dylan's genius with words, even when he was quite small. When Dylan first went up to London, he stayed with her only a short time because his meeting with Pamela and her mother, Amy Clotilda Johnson, and aunt proved so happy that he very shortly moved to their place at 53 Battersea Rise. Pamela Johnson has described that first meeting in February, 1934:

> He was nineteen, I was twenty-one. He arrived very late on a dull grey evening, and he was nervous, as I was. "It's nice to meet you after all those letters. Have you seen the Gauguins?" (He told me later that he had been preparing the remark about the Gauguins all the way from Swansea, and having made it, felt that his responsibility towards

a cultural atmosphere was discharged.)

He was very small and light. Under a raincoat with bulging pockets, one of which contained a quarter-bottle of brandy, another a crumpled mass of poems and stories, he wore a grey, polo-necked sweater, and a pair of very small trousers that still looked much too big on him. He had the body of a boy of fourteen. When he took off the pork-pie hat (which, he also told me later, was what he had decided poets wore) he revealed a large and remarkable head, not shaggy—for he was visiting —but heavy with hair the dull gold of threepenny bits springing in deep waves and curls from a precise middle parting. His brow was very broad, not very high: his eyes, the colour and opacity of caramels when he was solemn, the colour and transparency of sherry when he was lively, were large and fine, the lower rims rather heavily pigmented. His nose was a blob; his thick lips had a chapped appearance; a fleck of cigarette paper was stuck to the lower one. His chin was small, and the disparity between the breadth of the lower and upper parts of his face gave an impression at the same time comic and beautiful. He looked like a brilliant, audacious child, and at once my family loved and fussed over him as if he were one.

He stayed with us for a week or so on that occasion, for six weeks on the second, and for varying periods over a year or more. Gauguin wore off quickly. We walked over the Common on summer evenings to a little pub in Clapham Old Town, sometimes we took the bus to Chelsea—which seemed to us a cultural Mecca—and sat in the garden of the Six Bells, watching the little fountain drip onto its muddy stones, the men playing on the bowling green, which was still there in those days. I read his poems, and criticized them with a kind of bold reverence; he read mine, and criticized them by ridicule which was hilariously funny and also perfectly just. Sometimes we wrote doggerel poems together, in alternate lines.

At home, he liked my mother to type his stories

from his direction. Sometimes they were stories of inconceivable impropriety by anybody's standards—at that time. My mother (abandoning the keys): "Dylan, you cannot say that." Dylan, with a wave of the hand: "Put it in, Mrs. Johnson, just put it in. It's all right—I assure you, it's perfectly all right." [The story was an early draft of "The Burning Baby."]

In our quiet, middle-class neighbourhood, he not infrequently caused a stir; he meant to. I remember the disquiet of my aunt, one cold and foggy autumn morning, when she came downstairs to find Dylan about to go out into the busy main road wearing a blue and violet paisley dressing-gown that had once belonged to my six-foot uncle, and his own new, black, poetic felt hat. "Dylan! You can't go out like that! Come in at once!" Dylan: (raising the hat in respect and acquiescence): "Yes, Miss Howson. If you like. There may be something in what you say."[15]

The first visit was from February 23 to March 5, 1934. They went to see O'Casey's Within the Gates at the Royalty Theatre and enjoyed it enough to make a second visit. Later they went to see Franklin Dyall in The Merchant of Venice at the Alhambra Theatre and found it wonderfully funny. When Dyall delivered the line "I pray you, give me leave to go from hence, I am not well—" in the manner of someone in the throes of coronary thrombosis, they laughed so much, Pamela reported, they feared they would be thrown out of the theatre. In eleven days, the friendship had turned to romance; the correspondence that followed included love letters. At the same time the publication in The Listener on March 14 of Dylan's poem "Light Breaks Where No Sun Shines" had brought reactions of delight and dismay. The delight came from letters: Geoffrey Grigson asked if he would like to have some poems printed in New Verse; Stephen Spender said that he liked the poem and offered to get him some work doing reviews; T. S. Eliot invited him to call. The dismay came from the reactions of the less sophisticated of The Listener readers. A mass of letters came in complaining of the obscenity of some of the lines. One of the offending passages was

Nor fenced nor staked, the gushers of the sky
Spout to the rod divining in a smile
The oil of tears.

What Dylan referred to as "the smut-hounds" thought that he was
writing a "copulatory anthem." In reality, he explained to Pamela, it
was a metaphysical image of rain and grief. He denied the charges
of obscenity, but the BBC's Listener, at least for a while, boycotted all
of his poetry. Dylan announced that he would never darken their
doors again.

During his second visit with Pamela and her family—
March 31 to April 9—he attended his first literary luncheon, at the
Cafe Royal. Stephen Spender later reported that he was so nervous
in anticipation of the occasion that he had also invited William Plomer
to the luncheon. As it turned out, Spender and Plomer gossiped
together so avidly that Thomas was hardly drawn into the
conversation. But Dylan did begin reviewing books as a result of the
meeting, some for The Bookman and some for the Adelphi.

The romance flourished and Dylan wrote love letters
imagining their living together on an island in the Mediterranean
where they would write and read, love and sleep, singing their rhymes
to the seals. He believed with all his heart that they would live as
happily as the smile, which would never vanish, on the Cheshire face.
Along with this dream he recorded, with sadistic delight, the dreadful
things that would happen—a long future of bewilderment and
disillusion ending in Tax Collectors and their being forced to sell
matches. One day she would vomit at the sight of his face, and
he at the tones of her voice!

On reading the reviews of her book of poems
published as the first Referee prize, Symphony for Full Orchestra,
Pamela decided that she was no poet. But Dylan gave her sympathy;
he referred to the Times Literary Burblement and said that the offices
of that paper were peopled by old gentlemen who carried no literary
credentials but a long ruler to rap all originality over the knuckles, and
a pocket Tennyson as an infallible criterion to test everything they
reviewed. He told her that his father read the book and liked
it very much; but his own criticism of the poems continued, as
before, to be severe. And Pamela had already turned her attention
to composing a novel.

Dylan's third trip to London, June 13 to 27, was
followed by a fourth, August 10 to September 15, and by then it
seemed time for Pamela to be invited to Wales to meet his parents.
They went down to Wales together and, from September 15 to 28,
stayed at Cwmdonkin Drive, explored Rhossilli Bay, the Worm's Head
and Gower Peninsula. Dylan's father tried his hand at teaching
Pamela Welsh (something which Dylan had never learned), and

Pamela Hansford Johnson,
c. 1936

A photograph given by Dylan to Pamela,
c. 1935

Pamela Hansford Johnson, Aunt Pollie, Mrs. Thomas,
Uncle Dai and Aunt Dosie Rees, Uncle Bob, 1936

dismayed her by describing the medical procedures he had been undergoing in London for the treatment of throat cancer. For the young couple these were balmy happy days. Dylan was working on "Especially When the October Wind" and "Foster the Light," and preparing answers to an inquiry that was to appear in Grigson's New Verse in October. Pamela was finishing her rapidly written novel This Bed Thy Centre. And the romance prospered.

In the meantime, Dylan had himself won the second publication prize given by the Referee. But Faber & Faber, to whom the book had been offered, was slow to come to a decision and, after their several postponements, it was decided to withdraw the book from them. A willing publisher was found in the person of David Archer, co-owner of the Parton Bookshop. He was a friend of young poets, and himself contributed £20; Mark Goulden of the Sunday Referee contributed another £30; and the book appeared at the end of the year. Sheila MacLeod tells how she and Dylan's editor found the publisher:

> One foggy evening, making our slow way home from the Sunday Referee office, and while discussing Dylan's work and the second Book Prize, Victor Neuburg and I found ourselves in a fantastic cul-de-sac. Turning to regain the main thoroughfare we were arrested by a beam of light, suddenly raying out into the fog from a window down the alley. Fascinated, we retraced our steps to where all had been gloom, and stood enchanted before a magical bookshop in which seemed to be displayed most of the new books we had been yearning to buy.
>
> "Almost as if they expected us," Victor said as we walked in.
>
> The shop was empty and we hung over the books, while at the same time producing the sounds of customers needing attention. Soundlessly a strange young man, evidently the owner, seemed to have entered the shop from nowhere. He affected us as one whose personality was a little out of focus and strangely out of character with the books he stocked. After a difficult preliminary conversation, we bought the books we could least afford and asked the man whether by any chance Dylan Thomas had discovered this retreat. "It is known to all poets," David Archer said.[16]

Victor Neuburg's office was in his house in St. John's Wood and there in his garden young writers used to meet. Miss MacLeod has romantically recorded her first view of Dylan there with David Gascoyne, Beth Tregaskis, and a dozen others:

> I saw his bronze head of curls against a summer delphinium sky, with its drifting snow of clouds behind him: the head, then, of a handsome cherubic youth, crowned with an aura of thunderous power and doom. . . . To hear Victor Neuburg and Dylan conversing was like being present at the reunion of a young immature Jove, unaware of his powers, with the more remote fatherhood of older unknown Gods. Their play of trenchant wit and humour was like summer lightning, streaked with the forked incision of the older man.[17]

In the garden there would be al fresco tea, as the young writers sprawled on the grass with heaps of Cornish pasties and bottles of orange and lemon squash, a huge tree stump serving as a rostrum for the recital of improvised lyrics and argumentative exchanges. Dylan's attitude toward Victor Neuburg was not, as it turned out, very sympathetic. Before they met, Dylan explained in a letter to Pamela that Neuburg called himself "the Vicky-bird" because, parrotlike, he wanted repetitions of what he had had before. He said that Neuburg blabbed of some unsectarian region in the clouds where poetry reached its highest level and then ruined the truth of that by saying that the artist must, of necessity, preach socialism. Dylan went on to assert that there was no necessity for the artist to do anything, that he was a law unto himself: The only limitation an artist should submit to is the limitation of form. And in the case of poetry the form should arise out of the words; it should find itself and never be superimposed. As for his own aim in poetry he announced that he did not want to express only what other people feel, but that he wanted to rip something away and show what other people never see. He felt that Neuburg's muse was never drunk enough to be really emotional and never sober enough to be really intellectual. When Neuburg compared one of Pamela's poems to what Dylan considered to be a less worthy one, he complained that it was like comparing Milton with Stilton. And when Neuburg called his own poems experimentalist, he was furious. Dylan wrote a fierce denunciation of Neuburg to Pamela because he had been working with meticulous off-rhyme and within the most extreme restrictions of syllable-count.

One of Dylan's last adventures in Swansea was with

a local literary society. With all the bravado of his nineteen years he delivered a paper entitled "Pornography in Nineteenth Century Literature." Bert Trick has recounted this event:

> The invitation had come as a result of a young man who came to see me one Sunday evening. I had been writing a series of articles in one of the local papers suggesting certain socialist reforms. This young man had so misread the content of those articles that in his initial letter to me he suggested that I might think of taking the leadership in the local Moseleyite Party—the fascist Blackshirts. This amused Dylan so much that he said, "Oh, do invite the young man to your house on Sunday night, Bert, and we'll see what we can do to convert him." The fellow did turn up, and spent the whole of Sunday afternoon and until very late on Sunday night with Dylan and me. By the time he left, we had indeed changed his views. I saw quite a lot of this young man after that, and one time he approached me and asked whether I thought Dylan would be willing to read a paper to the John O'London's Literary Circle. "I shall at least ask him, but I have no idea whether he would be prepared to do such a thing." When I put the proposal to Dylan at his house on the usual Wednesday visit: "Oh, I should be delighted," and there was a look of fiendish glee in his face when he said it. For some weeks then he prepared notes for the talk he was going to give. He wrote the whole thing out in longhand in that meticulous crabbed handwriting of his, and every Wednesday he would read the further efforts he had made toward the whole dossier that he was going to give to this meeting. But it was so outrageous, so completely outrageous, that frankly I didn't believe that he would ever attempt to put it across. We used to laugh at the jokes, at the double meanings, the barely hidden bawdiness that filled the address. But in our laughing, we never thought that he would go the whole way.
>
> The night came. Six of us assembled at 69 Glanbrydan Avenue in high spirits. I lined them up like soldiers, "Right turn, quick march," and we

marched out of the house already uproarious at the
prospect to come. Our way led past the Westbourne
Hotel just opposite the General Hospital in St. Helen's
Road. Dylan felt that he must have a glass of beer
to brace himself before going along; so we all
tumbled into the public house and we had a few
rounds of beers. Now, although we were quite
unaware of the fact, it seems that the workers on
a major drainage scheme of the local Council had
dug a trench across the road in front of the hospital,
and had left only a very few red lamps to warn
pedestrians of its presence. Coming out of the
lighted Pub into the darkness, I didn't see this
obstacle and immediately pitched headlong into the
ditch. And since I had no time to warn the others,
they one by one piled in on top of me. This made us
more delighted than ever. We were covered with
gray clay. With great festoons like pancakes on our
shoes, we were a disreputable lot.[18]

The meeting was to be held over the ironmongery, St. Helen's Road,
in the home of the owners, the Bates'. The muddy gang was admitted
by an elegant Mrs. Bates, ushered up carpeted stairs, and presented
to a room where sat five men and some dozen ladies, all prim, all
clothed in dark colors.

Dylan reported in a section of a letter to Pamela
headed "John O'London's Circumcision" that he gave them the works.
The speech, received at first with a frosty silence, gradually
warmed the audience to a few titters as the wisecracks multiplied,
and when he concluded with a resounding "Let Copulation thrive!"
the audience was ready with questions. In the Communist Erewhon
he had postulated, would there be perversions? He told them that
what they considered perversions are, for the most part, healthy
aspects of sexual life. By what means, someone asked, would a woman
defend her honor in such a state? Tin drawers, he said. Do you
believe in birth control and legal abortion? The day these things
become legalized, he said, would go down as a French Letter day in
history. Dylan maintained to Pamela that before the evening was over
the middle-aged ladies, who would previously have been shocked by
the mention of pajamas, were gaily discussing whirler-sprays,
Lesbianism, sanitary napkins, and fornication.

Later, in a letter to Trick from London, Dylan
recalled the episode and asked if he had attended one of those

high-brow salons again. But he knew that, of course, he hadn't, because they probably now had a subdivision of the Society—the Anti-Thomas and Trick League—which would be presided over by a back-biting eunuch and a couple of embodied maidenheads.

Dylan's health in this period was not good. Throughout March, April, and May he was losing weight (he went from 122 to 112 pounds), he had headaches, could not sleep, and was pale and haggard. Dylan said that according to a local doctor the conditions of his lungs was so bad that he had only four more years to live. This phrase, and variations on it, was to be repeated to many people during the rest of his life, but there is no evidence that his death had anything to do with the condition of his lungs. The fact that he coughed endlessly like a sea-lion may have been related to the fact that he smoked some forty Players or Woodbines a day. He said that he had chain-smoked for nearly five years and now had been put on a pipe which he hated. He complained that he was unwell—a headache that lasted a fortnight and no sleep for longer than that. His own troubles seemed to be duplicated in the coughing sheep who grazed on the filled-in reservoir opposite his house before they were taken to the slaughterhouse. He thought that all the doomed creatures were consumptive. There was one coughing sheep, a particularly diseased one, that kept him awake half the night by its hacking. Sometimes he became a little fond of the idea of his "poetical disease." He wrote Pamela that he didn't think consumption had very much effect on what he wrote. Despite his uneasiness about his health, he was producing poetry at a great rate. Sometimes he would go out and spend the day writing on Rhossilli beach, sometimes at the family country center, Blaen-Cwm, a few miles from Llanstephan, more often in his "Glamorgan villa" on Cwmdonkin Drive. But he longed for a change of scenery. He had begun to hate his world: He was tired of narrowness, dirtiness and what he felt was the perpetual ugliness of the Welsh. He wanted to get away from pettiness at home and from the giggles of his small-minded relatives.

The frequent trips to London had made for his dissatisfaction with depression-haunted Swansea; he was depressed by the looks of hunger and despair on the faces about him. Wales was as hard hit in the twenties and thirties as any part of England: there were dole-queues, bankrupt villages, children searching for coal on the slagheaps, unused quarries, still pit-wheels, hewers squatting in the cut, sag-roofed factories, plumeless stacks, knots of idle men outside the grim Employment Exchange. Out-of-work miners, out-of-work tin-platers, out-of-work everyone—even Dylan Thomas. As he later put it in a story, "Young Mr. Thomas was at the moment without employment, but it was understood that he would soon be leaving for London to make a career in Chelsea as a free-lance journalist; he was penniless, and hoped, in a vague way, to live on women."

In Chelsea

When he was ready to ascend to London in the second week of November, 1934, he made the automobile trip with his friend Fred Janes and Janes' parents. Fred, older than Dylan and ahead of him at school, had already attended the Royal College of Art in London. They had first met in 1931 at Warmley, Dan Jones' house in Sketty, when Fred was down on holiday. He was an earnest boy and a serious student of art, and the elder Thomases trusted him as a proper companion for Dylan. For the drive to London, Dylan wore his fashionable pork-pie hat and an enormous checked overcoat that looked, according to Fred Janes, like a tent over his slight body.

In London he did not find money easy to come by, but his mother was able to send him a pound a week, and as soon as he began reviewing novels he discovered that he could sell his review copies—sometimes twice. He occasionally sold them as soon as he got them and then, pleading loss, requested a second set from the publishers. He was not always very prompt in turning in his share of the rent. For this Fred Janes had a solution. When Dylan would plead that he had no money, Fred would simply get up first in the morning, grab Dylan's trousers, and turn them upside down until whatever coins were in them fell out. An enthusiast for calisthenics and weight-lifting, Janes was considerably stronger than Dylan. And he used to amuse himself by holding Dylan up in the air until he screamed to be let down.

In London, of course, he immediately saw Pamela, and then began their intense discussions—to marry or not to marry. One moment they would be ready to go down to the registry office, the next moment there were reconsiderations. Finally the decision came. Dylan, in Pamela's words, wanted someone a bit more "with it," Pamela someone a bit less. And thus the romance ended, in the fall of 1934, but not the friendship. They continued to see one another in London and in the summer of 1936 when she made a trip to Wales. But in December, 1936, Pamela married Gordon (Neil) Stewart, and thereafter they met less often.

The reason for their separating was apparently

Dylan's increasing bohemianism. Even before he had left Swansea he had sown his first really wild oats. He had written to Pamela an agonized confession saying that he could hardly hold the pencil or see the paper. He compared his state to the time when he said good-by to her for the first time: It was in a London Kardomah cafe when he felt the sensation of loving her so much that he was unable to tell her. Now, too, he felt as if his nerves were so exacerbated that he was on the point of breaking into little bits. He didn't know if he were shouting or whispering when he spoke. He knew that she would be terribly angry with him and that perhaps she would never write to him again, but he wanted to tell her the honest truth.

His confession was of an excursion out on the Gower Peninsula. He had been drinking a lot in Laugharne and feeling a bit odd even then. On a Wednesday morning he went down to a bungalow in Gower to stay with a drinking companion named Cliff. That evening, at the pub, they were joined by a young lady who for present purposes can be called Jane, who was tall and thin and dark, with a loose red mouth, a harsh sort of laugh. On the way home she made persistent advances to both of the boys, all of them rather drunk. Once at the bungalow and after a few more drinks, they retired. Cliff decided, as Dylan put it, "very modernly" to sleep with Jane. No sooner had he got in bed with her, however, than she screamed and ran into Dylan's. They slept together not only that night but for the next three nights, and the drinking continued day and night. Confessing everything in detail, he announced that he was on the border of D.T.s and insisted that he was still deeply in love with Pamela and that he desperately hoped that she would forgive him.

In London the bohemian life continued. Many years later Dylan recalled these days on a television program that featured the paintings of Fred Janes. Portraits of the four participants, painted by Janes, were projected upon the screen, and immediately after the showing of the portrait, the subject appeared and spoke impromptu. In his turn Dylan said:

> It was a terrible long time ago. Before television.
> . . . Before the radio even, I shouldn't be surprised
> when I see that dewy goblin portrait frog-goggling at
> me out of the past. (I think that portrait must have
> been losing weight: I can hardly recognise it now.)
> Before the internal-combustion engine, before the
> invention of the wheel, oh what a long nice time
> ago, in the Golden Days. Do you remember then,

Fred? The Golden Days, in London, when we were
exiled bohemian boily boys. There were three of
us then: you and me, and Mervyn Levy, three very
young monsters green and brimming from Swansea,
stiff with lyrics and ambitions and still lifes, all
living together in one big bare barmy beautiful
room kept by a Mrs. Parsnip, as far as I can
remember, in Redcliffe Gardens. Two of us had
beards, and I grew one too, sparse and ginger and
limp, like a depressed marmalade cat's with the
mange; I don't know what happened to it; either it
fell off, or was blown off, or it just grew in, I can't
remember. Mervyn had a different beard every
fortnight, and every one his own: spade-shaped,
Assyrian, Captain Kettle, Victorian-celebrity, rabbi,
Uncle Sam goatee, Southern Gentleman, goat; and
once he had only half a beard, oiled and curled and
scented, on one side of his face; but nobody seemed
to notice in that neighbourhood, which was
infuriating. Mrs. Parsnip was always boiling cabbage
downstairs, cabbage and lights and, maybe, mice;
and one of us was painting mackerel mackerel
all the time, day in day out, the same mackerel too,
until they used to get up and walk around the room,
just like real live models; and the chimney huffed and
puffed like a wolf; and I think there were tomcats
lodging in the next room: perhaps they paid their
rent with mice to Mrs. Parsnip, for boiling. Upstairs,
right above us, small desperate men were composing
an opera, or so we believed, a rather unmusical
opera heavily dependent on screams and the
throwing of buckets; and there was another lodger,
too, who used to live in a little leaking room off
the stairs: we never saw him, but he used to make
a noise like a train going through a tunnel. Mervyn
Levy was an art student, and just beginning other
experiments, Janes was practising mackerel and
jujitsu; and I was writing poems (of a kind) for
immortality and the Poets' Corner of the Sunday
Referee. What we cooked, I don't know, unless it was
our next-door neighbours, miaows and all, but it
tasted like the Ritz. There was no weather in these

Mervyn Levy by Alfred Janes

Dylan by Alfred Janes

Golden Days, only light and dark, loud and soft,
miserable and bouncing. We hadn't got any money at
all, and to show you how young we were, even that
was delightful: or is this middle-age talking, looking
back through a ring-o'-roses?

Well, anyway, there we were. That's when the
portrait of me, a frog in his salad days, was painted.
And those were the days that, now, we get so
nostalgic about. But in those London days, I
remember, we were terribly nostalgic, too, about our
town, Swansea, that we had left for ever and
for ever.[19]

The digs Dylan and Janes shared consisted of one unfurnished room
on Redcliffe Street in South Kensington in a house owned by a
Mrs. Heather. The room had a pair of camp beds, a table, and an oven
that looked like a biscuit tin which functioned over a single gas ring.
Janes was the chef and his specialty was a huge pancake made
of boiled onions and potatoes. The makeshift clothes closet was an
old iron bedstead, stood on end and covered with a castoff curtain.
Fred had made an easel of the only chair in the room so that anyone
who wanted to sit was obliged to use one of the cots. How sturdy
these were Dylan's father found out one day when, on a visit, he sat
down only to have everything give way beneath him.

Dylan wrote to Bert Trick that he was living in the
quarter of the pseudo-artists, of the beards, where people cultivated
the naughty expressions of outmoded periods and where he attended
Bohemian parties more boring than he would ever have thought
possible. He made fun of everyone's being slightly drunk, slightly
dirty, slightly wicked, slightly crazed, and he made fun of himself for
repeating platitudes on Gauguin and Van Gogh as though they were
the most original things in the world.

From Mrs. Heather's house, the two boys moved to
No. 21 Coleherne Road—a little nearer the heart of Chelsea, where
they were joined by the third Swansea boy, Mervy Levy. Like Fred,
Mervyn was a painter, and had known Dylan ever since the dame
school days of Mirador Crescent. But the personalities of the two
young painters were very different. Fred was the responsible one, the
one who did the cooking and paid the rent. Mervyn was the true
bohemian: when he didn't have any funds he would rip his already
ragged trousers even further and, disguised as a beggar, stand on a
street corner until he had enough money for a few beers. And he wore
the luxuriant succession of beards Dylan described. Dylan relied on

Fred to provide a steady center for his life in London; he relied on
Mervyn for the clown companionship he loved. Dylan as a young man
could assume a remarkable resemblance to Harpo Marx—the crown
of light curls, the full face, the falsely innocent eyes. Mervy, with a
fine talent for mimicry, could transform himself at a moment's notice
into a replica of Groucho. Their Marx Brothers routine gave new life
to many a sagging party.

Dylan extricated himself from many a difficult
situation by his personal charm. One night some time later, when
Levy was living elsewhere, Dylan arrived for a visit with a friend—both
of them drunk and roaring. The rather proper landlady came to Levy.
"Some disgraceful men are downstairs asking for you," she said.
"I wish you would send them away." When Levy came downstairs
with the landlady, Dylan saw the fire in her eyes. He began covering
her arms gallantly with kisses from the fingers to the elbow,
whereupon she broke into smiles and welcomed him in. On another
occasion when a policeman approached Dylan and his friend Anthony
Hubbard for creating a disturbance and was about to haul them in,
Dylan dropped to his knees. "O, Mr. Policeman, please be a neece
man," he chanted. The policeman laughed, melted, and sent them on
their way. About another occasion, Mervyn Levy later wrote,

> Wandering the streets we wove incredible
> fantasies as we often did when we were together for
> a while. How many mice would it take to pull the
> London to Glasgow Express? Half a million? A
> million? Oh! more, lots more! Don't forget they'd
> have to pull it at the same speed as it normally goes.
> Anyway if you had enough mice you could do it. It
> stood to reason. But you would have to lay special
> mouse-tracks (we discussed their character). And
> the mice, of course, would need egging-on. But how?
> Cats? No, they would make the mice hysterical. It
> would be essential to keep strict order. Well, then,
> thousands of midgets with whips stationed at
> intervals along the tracks? Yes, that seemed the most
> likely answer. Could you do it with worms? With five
> hundred billion of these struggling, squelching,
> loathsome creatures? If you had enough, yes,
> obviously.[20]

On one occasion, traveling together in a taxi through London, Dylan
snuggled his thin body down into a vast overcoat, pulled his hat down
and, grinning through his broken teeth, muttered delightedly, "I love

it here, Mervy; it's like a womb with a view." Sometimes at night, when Dylan was tired and low, he would say, "Mervy, sing me to sleep." And Mervyn would get out his guitar and sing in a sweet voice the old ballad of the "Bandalero": "For I am waiting and watching, an outlaw defiant; for I am waiting and watching for ransom or spy."

A major reason for Dylan's move to London was to be there when his book appeared in December. A very small book of only eighteen poems, nearly all of them difficult to comprehend, by a writer known only to a limited circle, is likely to be ignored, but Dylan's first book was warmly reviewed. Rayner Heppenstall wrote in the Adelphi:

> Nearly all poetry is bad today because poets are either too unsociable or too weak-kneed to get up on their hind legs and perform. . . . I recognise in Dylan Thomas a poet so free from embarrassment, sore throat, sulks and stutters, that I must formally declare his 18 Poems the most hopeful thing in English poetry since Robert Graves' last volume. . . . Faults? Plenty. . . . Some lushness, clash, and confusion of images, straining to make words do more than words can, constriction. . . . But these phenomena all come from the virtue of an overfertile imagination. . . . You ought to read this book.[21]

And in The Listener, the eminent poet and critic Edwin Muir wrote: "The first thing that strikes one about Mr. Dylan Thomas' poetry is its purely poetic force: there is nothing in it that could be taken for prose: his thought seems to transmute itself naturally and continuously into imagery."[22]

Both Bert Trick and John Jennings wrote highly favorable reviews in the Swansea and West Wales Guardian, but Dylan was annoyed by the exaggerated praise of 18 Poems Trevor Hughes wrote in a letter to the same paper. Dylan called it mannered blarney, and damned his reference to buds and blossoms which seemed to make him into something in a vase. Somewhat surprisingly, the sharpest criticism appeared in the magazine New Verse, whose editor had until then been his chief champion. Geoffrey Grigson had published five of the poems in this book, and was to publish four more that would be included in Dylan's second book, but in his review he found more to criticize than to praise. He objected to the rhythmic, thematic, verbal, and imaginative monotonies. He felt the "birth, copulation, death" themes were repeated too often in a vocabulary

Edith Sitwell

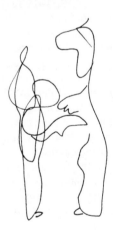

Queen Edith Sitwell & Princess Marianne Moore on her first meeting

Dylan's doodle of Sitwell and Moore

drawn too much from the anatomic world. But, he concluded: "take away what is bad and the good remnants are these: a rhetorical toughness, the now rare intellectual virtue of an attempt at form, occasional but not infrequent excellences of imaginative statement and expression of reality beyond reality. . . . He needs severity from himself; but he has more inside him and a more sceptical intelligence and writes more genuine prose (not to include poems) than most new poets."[23]

The really clinching praise came later from Edith Sitwell in the February, 1936, issue of the London Mercury. "It would be impossible to exaggerate my feeling of excitement when I read this poem ["A Grief Ago," a poem not included in 18 Poems, but which appeared in the October, 1935, issue of Programme], so beautiful and moving for all its obscurities. Here, I said to myself, is a young man who has every likelihood of becoming a great poet, if only he will work hard enough at subduing his obscurity. I know of no young poet of our time whose poetic gifts are on such great lines."[24] Dylan Thomas' reputation was established and was later confirmed in the high praise repeated when Miss Sitwell reviewed the Twenty-Five Poems in the fall of 1936 in the Sunday Times.

In the winter of 1934–1935, Dylan found many good friends in London—the Scots poet and critic Ruthven Todd, the poet Bernard Spencer, the Welsh painter William Scott (who lived upstairs at Coleherne Road), the poet and ad-writer Norman Cameron, and the book-page editor of the Morning Post as well as of New Verse, Geoffrey Grigson. He would stay now with one and now with another, earning some £5 a week by reviewing current mystery thrillers for the Post. And he lived the emancipated life of a twenty-year-old just up from the provinces—making pals of easy girls and drinking prodigally. Grigson tells of one of their typical fantasies:

> Serial jokes and myths—word jokes and word myths—ran through our association as they run in families; especially a serial myth of advertisements for night custard, a Thomas invention and patent, an alchemical liquid almost, which satisfied, with every obscene twist, that "night starvation" already postulated, with Cameron's help (since he was a copywriter), in the advertisements for one of those beverages you drink hot before going to bed.[25]

Dylan acquired all sorts of nicknames: The Disembodied Gland, Ditch, The Ugly Suckling, Dirty Dylan. He seldom opened books now (except for the thrillers) and he had abandoned his esthetic necktie. Instead he adopted a pose, which London seemed to prefer, as the Toughish Boy, the Boy with a Load of Beer. From time to time he would spit up blood. While he was fearful about his state of health, he also used to dramatize it. As one of his friends put it, he was "a bit in love with the traditional idea of the Young Poet with V.D., or the Young Poet with T.B."

In Donegal

To get away from his raffish London life and to work seriously on a new book of poems J. M. Dent had offered to publish, he went off with Geoffrey Grigson for some weeks in the summer of 1935 to the west coast of Ireland. En route they stopped for a few days with Dan Jones in Harrow. Jones had left the Grammar School in 1931 and gone on to the University College of Swansea, where he had read English and gained his B.A. in 1934. Between 1931 and 1934 he had set a great many of Dylan's poems to music, music that has been described as highly romantic and at times florid. He was to attend the Royal Academy of Music in 1935–1936 and to win a Mendelssohn Scholarship which would enable him to live in Rome and Vienna in 1936–1937. Dylan reported that in the summer of 1935 he was cleverer than ever. He wrote that Dan Jones wasn't sure either of music or writing, though he did both competently and often brilliantly. But he said he liked him despite the fact that he was a prig, a snob, and a boor.

Grigson and Dylan then made their way on to Glen Lough, a lovely valley between Ardara and Killybegs at Nina Cross, Liod, County Donegal, where they lived on the farm of Dan Ward in a kind of shed perched on a hill facing the wild Atlantic. Here there had once been a three-room cottage in which, according to legend, Bonnie Prince Charlie had hidden out. The original house had fallen into ruins, and it had been discovered in 1926 by the American artist Rockwell Kent who, with his wife, had repaired the surviving shed (once a shelter for animals) and made it into a sleeping room and studio. They had whitewashed the place, added homemade furniture, and decorated it with calico, to turn it into "the little house" in which they lived for a year and then abandoned. Geoffrey Grigson later wrote:

> It was in that shed, on the edge of a small stream
> from the lakes, that Dylan and I lived for a while,
> building turf fires to dry ourselves out and keeping
> a quart bottle of potheen—illegal, colourless whisky

—hidden in a potato patch outside, below a lushness of chickweed. If indeed he had been in danger of TB, I daresay he ought not to have been in the dampness and softness of Ireland; but here he was drinking less potheen, at any rate, than he had drunk of beer and spirits in London, and less porter than milk and buttermilk.

The Swansea Changeling, who might at any time go back to his people, waded through mixed flames of loosestrife and corn marigold which floored the valley. From the cliffs he watched gannets drop and fleck the Atlantic; or climbing steeply to the lakes at the back of the farm and the converted stable, we shouted up to the surrounding ringing mountains We are the Dead, for the multiple echo to reply in sequence We are the Dead, the Dead, the Dead, the Dead. We shouted to these mountains above the lake one evening till we frightened ourselves, stumbling down afterwards through heather and fern and sog to the comfort of the cottage, where Dylan stretched stained white feet, Swansea feet, to the warm turf, alongside the brown, huge feet of the farmer Dan Ward. At times we sneaked down the enormous cliffs to a cold soul-tightening ocean and sang the "Ram of Derbyshire" to black seals. There was no sand, no gravel, below these cliffs, only white pebbles shaped like eggs or heads by Brancusi. We drew faces on them with black crayon, we named them, set them against rock, and cracked them, with fling after fling of other huge white pebbles, into literary nothingness —since the faces were of authors—and literary oblivion.[26]

The fact that the faces were of friends and patrons (Edith Sitwell and Cyril Connolly) as well as enemies gave the sport a special fillip.

After a week Grigson returned to London to his wife and small daughter, leaving Dylan, who planned to stay until September. Dylan's routine was to rise at nine, breakfast and clean up till ten, and read or write until one. After lunch he would walk over the cliffs to the sea and stay there till nearly four. Back at the shed, he would make himself some creamy tea, then write until early dusk. There would be a climb over the hills to the high lakes where he would fish until dark, and then back home for supper and bed.

He grew a very thick, very curly ginger-colored Assyrian beard, "neatly regular, sweetly disorderly," which he rather fancied; and the poems were coming nicely. There was potheen with supper, and from time to time he would walk the miles over to Glendrumakie where there was a shop and a bar.

He wrote to Bert Trick that he was in a wild country where there were gannets and seals and puffins flying and puffing and playing outside his window. There were great rocks petrified like the old Fates and Destinies of Ireland; there were the smooth white pebbles like the souls of the dead Irish. And he told how he had forced the dead Irish to answer in echoes from behind the hill that they were sad, gray, lost, forgotten, and damned forever.

Dan Ward, the farmer, and his Gaelic-speaking wife Rose had felt Dylan's magnetism and had been kind to him, to their cost. One day Dylan picked up and walked over the mountains and away without paying them a penny of the agreed sum for his food and lodging. The money was finally paid by one of Dylan's friends. Confronted with his misbehavior, he reacted as he often did under such circumstances by pouting and, as Grigson put it, "acting the injured Suckling."

During the fall and winter in London Dylan reviewed mystery thrillers for the Morning Post and succeeded in placing his creative work in a variety of publications: poems appeared in the Oxford Programme, the Majorca Caravel, Comment, Scottish Bookman, and Purpose; stories appeared in Comment and Life and Letters Today. He was seeing Hugh Porteous, Oswell Blakeston, Geoffrey Grigson, William Empson, and, most frequently, Norman Cameron. He had lunch with T. S. Eliot and found him charming and unaffected—they discussed various methods of curing rheumatism. "I think it was in 1927 I had my worst bout," said Eliot, "and I tried Easu Ointment." Later when someone suggested a call on Eliot, Dylan said, "You mean the Archbishop? I wouldn't dare." But he did dare, and Eliot gave him a substantial sum of money.

Dylan dramatized the way of his life in London as promiscuity, booze, coloured shirts, too much talk, too little work. In March, 1936, once again to get away from it all, he accepted the invitation of Mrs. Wyn Henderson to be "mascot and very welcome guest" in Cornwall. Mrs. Henderson, the manager of Peggy Guggenheim's Bloomsbury art gallery, the Guggenheim Jeune, had a cottage at Polgigga, Porthcurno, a tiny place between Penzance and Land's End. Life there was not conducive to pub-crawls, since the nearest pub was three miles away, and it was conducive to work for there was little else to do. Dylan seemed to his hostess to be touchingly clothes-conscious; he liked to wear a handsome sweater his mother had knitted for him with the flamboyant scarf that had belonged to his sister. He worked steadily on poems and stories, and, at the persuasion of Mrs. Henderson, listened to records. He was not especially moved by music, but at Easter he did hear through the St. Matthew Passion which, he said, he found to be a wonderful and at the same time very homosexual love story. When Mrs. Henderson and her mother moved to Mousehole, Dylan went along, and there found his old friends the painters William Scott and Alfred Janes. At the house there were many talks about psychology, because Mrs. Henderson, having just undergone a Freudian analysis of several years duration, had many observations to make about the motivations for some of Dylan's eccentric behavior. With this intellectual analysis of the unconscious, Dylan would have nothing to do.

Surrealism

One of the signal events for all artistic London in the summer of 1936 was the International Surrealist Exhibition held June 11 to July 4 in the vast halls of the New Burlington Galleries. This show had been organized on the initiative of Roland Penrose, assisted by the poet David Gascoyne and many others, including Henry Moore, Herbert Read, André Breton, Salvador Dali, Paul Nash, and Paul Eluard. Dali had arranged to have an attractive young lady cover her face completely with roses and, on opening day, to circulate among the guests as a flower-headed woman. Dylan was delighted with this and other surrealist manifestations and returned to see the show several times. Older London was considerably upset: the periodical Studio felt that the show "called for severe criticism." But younger London, including Dylan and his friends, loved the nonsense of Dali in his diving suit and the other absurdities. On one of his visits, Dylan is said to have joined in the spirit of the exhibition by boiling string and serving it daintily to those present. On June 26 there was a poetry evening in the Galleries on which Paul Eluard, David Gascoyne, Dylan, and others recited their poems. Dylan's poetic instincts were as far as could be from surrealist automatism, but, while he had his own obsessive need to revise and to concentrate on formal elements, he was fascinated with the surrealists' extraordinary images from the unconscious. His own surrealism was most prominent in the stories that had begun to appear

Garden of Richard Hughes' home by Laugharne Castle

as early as March, 1934, when "After the Fair" was printed in the New English Weekly. Thereafter his stories, expressing varying degrees of fantastic imagination, appeared in a variety of publications: New Stories, Adelphi, Janus, Transition, Comment, Yellow Jacket, Seven, and two each in New English Weekly, Criterion, and Wales, and three each in Life and Letters Today and Contemporary Poetry and Prose; their first appearance in book form came in The Map of Love, published by Dent in 1939.

Caitlin Macnamara

Dylan first met his future wife in April of 1936 in a Charlotte Street pub in London, the Wheatsheaf. There was a large loud party going on which included Augustus John who was there in the company of Caitlin Macnamara, a twenty-two year old neighbor of his who had been sitting for a portrait in his studio at Fryern Court, Hampshire. Almost instantly, on meeting, Dylan and Caitlin found themselves attracted to one another: they talked for hours and planned quickly to meet again. A few weeks later the couple were invited by the novelist Richard Hughes to visit him in his house beside the ruined castle of Laugharne in Wales. Dylan and Caitlin accepted with delight, and what began as a weekend went on and on and on—because the pair had no money to leave. Thus began the attachment that was to lead, about a year later, to their marriage.

Caitlin Macnamara's antecedents were French and Irish. Her paternal grandfather, a landowner with large estates in Ennistymon, was for a time High Sheriff of County Clare; her paternal grandmother was the youngest daughter of Sir Alfred Cooper, who had been a government administrator in Australia. Her father, Francis Macnamara, was able to live for a good part of his life on an inheritance. His early ambition was to become a barrister, but he soon abandoned this in favor of writing. He wrote stories and published one book of his poems, Marionettes. An expert yachtsman who designed his own boats, he was a good-looking man of great charm, noted for his exercise of the Irish gift of gab. Augustus John used to say that Francis Macnamara was the most brilliant man he had ever met. Sometime after he inherited Ennistymon House from his father, he turned it into a hotel called The Falls which he ran successfully for some years, and then sold. He died in 1946.

Caitlin's maternal great-grandfather, Edouard

Majolier, came from Congenies (Gard), France, to marry the daughter of an English publisher and become a naturalized Englishman. Her London grandfather, Edouard Majolier, married Susanna Cooper of Clarina, County Limerick. Their daughter, Yvonne Majolier, Caitlin's mother, grew up in London and Congenies, the family village near Nimes. She met Francis Macnamara in London and they were married there in 1907 and had four children: John, born in 1908, Nicolette, born in 1911, who became a novelist and wife of the painter Anthony Devas; and Brigit, born in 1912. Caitlin, the fourth and last of the children, was born in the Macnamara house at 12 Hammersmith Terrace in London on December 8, 1913.

Shortly after Caitlin's birth, the family broke up by common agreement. Mr. Macnamara wished to be undistracted by the children and to attend to his literary aspirations. Mrs. Macnamara chose to lead her own life, and in 1923 moved with the children to New Inn House in Blashford, near Ringwood, in the New Forest, Hampshire. The four children were brought up by a governess. For a year Caitlin attended the Grovely Manor school in the Shelley House in Bournemouth. The liveliest of the four children, she was fond of riding, swimming, and dancing. Like the other children, she was brought up to speak French as well as English. Uninfluenced by her father, who disapproved of religion on principle, she was routinely admitted to the Church of England.

Asserting herself in a dramatic way, Caitlin at seventeen joined her school friend Vivian John, the youngest daughter of their neighbor Augustus John, and ran away from home to London to go on the stage. Their first move was to take dancing lessons: tap, softshoe, and the rest. At the age of eighteen, Caitlin was a member of the chorus line on the stage of the Palladium. If her dancing was good, her punctuality clearly was not; after about two months her professional stage career was ended by the management. Her interest in dancing, however, persisted. She met an exotic Polishwoman who taught "eurhythmic" dancing, and a number of photographs exist giving proof of her feeling for the style. She has referred to this period as "my halcyon Isadora Duncan days, when I chose to fancy myself as flowing with melody, movement, and everything but the kitchen sink, including Grecian draperies, and Mercurian sandals, no half measures for me." Her career as a dancer might have led to her becoming one of the Blue Bell Girls: an impresario came through London collecting chorus girls to take to Paris, and Caitlin was excited by the notion of dancing at the Moulin Rouge. But aspirants under the age twenty-one had to have

Eurhythmic dancing by Caitlin

Caitlin Macnamara by Augustus John

Home of Yvonne Macnamara, Blashford, Ringwood

parental permission, and this Mrs. Macnamara refused.

Dylan later said that he and Caitlin had been planning to marry from the first day they met. In the summer of 1937 they went to Cornwall together, stayed in a Newlyn studio for a few weeks, and then moved to Wyn Henderson's "Lobster Pot" on Mousehole harbor. There they made the final decision, and on July 12, 1937, they were married in the registry office of Penzance in Cornwall. They continued staying with Mrs. Henderson for a while, and then Augustus John came down and drove them to Swansea for a visit with Dylan's parents. Later they proceeded to Ringwood, where they settled in with Caitlin's mother.

Mrs. Macnamara's house, the New Inn House, a charming old place at a fork in the road called Blashford, lies just outside the market town of Ringwood, Hampshire. Once it was a farm. Fields around the house are rambling flower gardens. Before its days as a farmhouse, more than a hundred years ago, it was a pub— The New Inn—and the public room, with its bay window, now serves as the family dining room. At the rear there is a modern addition—a woodshed converted into a one-story large rectangular room, the Big Room, with a writing table in front of a large window looking onto one section of the garden. It was in this studio room that Dylan worked and reworked many poems: "We lying by seasand," "I make this in a warring absence," "The spire cranes," and "O make me a mask." Here he wrote such prose as "The Map of Love," "In the Direction of the Beginning," the "Tribute to Auden," and many fiction reviews for the New English Weekly. Dylan used to go off to the Big Room to work every afternoon. After finishing a revision of a poem and making a fresh copy of the new version, he would turn the discarded bits into tight rolls, and by the end of the afternoon the floor would be covered with tightly rolled pieces of paper.

It was a period of no money and great happiness. Every day he and Caitlin used to ride on bicycles into the New Forest, to Bluebell Wood, out onto Cuckoo Hill. "We are quiet and small and cigarette-stained," he wrote, "and very young. I've read two dozen thrillers, the whole of Jane Austen, a new Wodehouse, some old Powys, a book of Turgenev, three lines of Gertrude Stein, and an anthology of Pure Poetry by George Moore. There are only about 2,000 books left in the house."[27]

Here Dylan completed one of his best-known works— a lament for his Aunt Annie Jones, who died February 7, 1933. Originally it had only twenty-four lines and was a generalized lament; later it was turned into a personal elegy. It lay in

Dylan and Caitlin

"In loving memory of Annie Jones,
Mount Pleasant, Llangain,
died 7 Feb. 1933, 70 years old. Also
her husband James Jones,
died 3 Sept. 1942, 78 years old."

Dylan and his mother
at Capel Newydd, Llanybri

Dylan and Caitlin

his notebook with all the others until he decided to publish the volume <u>The Map of Love</u>. On April 1, 1938, he sent fifteen lines of it to Vernon Watkins. "I knew it was feeble," he said, "as it stood before, & the end of it—that is the part that becomes the new brackets —was too facile &, almost, grandiosely sentimental. (By the way, when you type it, will you spell Anne as Ann: I just remember that's the right way: she was an ancient peasant aunt.) I think there are some good lines, but don't know about the thing as a whole."[28]

When he had made his final revision, he called Caitlin and Mrs. Macnamara out into the garden, and there in the summerhouse read it to them:

After the Funeral

(In memory of Ann Jones)

After the funeral, mule praises, brays,
Windshake of sailshaped ears, muffle-toed tap
Tap happily of one peg in the thick
Grave's foot, blinds down the lids, the teeth in black,
The spittled eyes, the salt ponds in the sleeves,
Morning smack of the spade that wakes up sleep,
Shakes a desolate boy who slits his throat
In the dark of the coffin and sheds dry leaves,
That breaks one bone to light with a judgment clout,
After the feast of tear-stuffed time and thistles
In a room with a stuffed fox and a stale fern,
I stand, for this memorial's sake, alone
In the snivelling hours with dead, humped Ann
Whose hooded, fountain heart once fell in puddles
Round the parched worlds of Wales and drowned each sun
(Though this for her is a monstrous image blindly
Magnified out of praise; her death was a still drop;
She would not have me sinking in the holy
Flood of her heart's fame; she would lie dumb and deep
And need no druid of her broken body).
But I, Ann's bard on a raised hearth, call all
The seas to service that her wood-tongued virtue
Babble like a bellbuoy over the hymning heads,
Bow down the walls of the ferned and foxy woods
That her love sing and swing through a brown chapel,
Bless her bent spirit with four, crossing birds.

Her flesh was meek as milk, but this skyward statue
With the wild breast and blessed and giant skull
Is carved from her in a room with a wet window
In a fiercely mourning house in a crooked year.
I know her scrubbed and sour humble hands
Lie with religion in their cramp, her threadbare
Whisper in a damp word, her wits drilled hollow,
Her fist of a face died clenched on a round pain;
And sculptured Ann is seventy years of stone.
These cloud-sopped, marble hands, this monumental
Argument of the hewn voice, gesture and psalm,
Storm me forever over her grave until
The stuffed lung of the fox twitch and cry Love
And the strutting fern lay seeds on the black sill.

In Wales

As might have been predicted, there was a sympathy between Dylan
and such a free spirit as Lawrence Durrell. The two men first met in
December, 1937, when Dylan and Caitlin were in London staying for a
while with the formidable Anna Wickham, a poetess intimidating both
in size and forthrightness. Durrell had come from Paris to seek out
Miss Wickham because he had heard that she was keeping an
"interesting" diary, parts of which might be regarded as actionable
if published in England. This made it potentially suitable for Booster,
the iconoclastic magazine Durrell and Henry Miller were publishing in
Paris. It turned out that there was no diary, but the introduction of
the two men on that occasion led to Dylan's saying that he would like
very much to meet Henry Miller. Later, in correspondence, Durrell
tried to persuade Dylan to visit Greece at the time Miller was going
to be there. But Dylan knew where he could write best. He told Durrell

> I think England is the very place for a fluent and fiery
> writer. The highest hymns of the sun are written in
> the dark. I like the grey country. A bucket of Greek
> sun would drown in one colour the crowds of
> colours I like trying to mix for myself out of a grey
> flat insular mud. If I went to the sun I'd just sit
> in the sun; that would be very pleasant but I'm not
> doing it, and the only necessary things I do are the
> things I am doing.[29]

Later, when Booster was threatened with action for obscenity and the
magazine was transferred to London under the name of Delta, Dylan

did meet Miller and liked him; but when finally Dylan moved from England, it was not to Greece but back to Wales.

Dylan and Caitlin left Ringwood for a period of seven months: in April, 1938, they moved first to the home of his parents in Bishopston, a suburb of Swansea out on the Gower Peninsula where Mr. and Mrs. Thomas had retired when the elder Thomas left teaching in 1937. After about three months there, they moved on to Laugharne, the village of their early romance. They first took "an ugly furnished fisherman's cottage" on Gosport Street, then moved to Sea View, "a tall and dignified house at the posh end of town," where they were to live on and off for the next three or four years. The house is just one room deep, although it has a basement and is three stories high. (A memento of their residence is visible to this day: Just inside the front door is a small hallway and stairs down to the kitchen; on the ceiling of the staircase in Dylan's neat, careful handwriting one can read "Caitlin and Dylan Thomas began living here August, 1938.") The tiny rooms were snug and suited Dylan's love for coziness. He once said

> I'm not a country man; I stand for, if anything, the aspidistra, the provincial drive, the morning cafe, the evening pub; I'd like to believe in the wide open spaces as the wrapping around walls, the windy boredom between house and house, hotel and cinema, bookshop and tube-station; man made his house to keep the world and the weather out, making his own weathery world inside. . . .[30]

In the years at Sea View, the couple lived close to poverty (despite the fact that they had the services of a maid) because there was really no steady income. "Last year at this time," Dylan wrote, "Caitlin and I were doing an act in a garret. This time we're just as poor, or poorer, but the ravens—soft, white, silly ravens—will feed us."

During the stay in Bishopston and the residence at Sea View, Dylan's friendship with Vernon Watkins was renewed. Some eight years older, Watkins had been a poet before he met Dylan, although his first book was not published until 1941. In the spring of 1935, having seen the 18 Poems in a bookshop, the twenty-nine-year-old Vernon Watkins left an invitation at Cwmdonkin Drive for Dylan to drop by when he next returned from London. Of that meeting Watkins wrote "He was slight, . . . shy, rather flushed and eager in manner, deep-voiced, restless, humorous, with large, wondering, yet acutely intelligent eyes, gold curls, snub nose, and the

Sea View, Laugharne

Laugharne Main Street

Vernon Watkins by Alfred Janes

Dylan and Caitlin

Croquet at Vernon Watkins', Pennard Cliffs, Gower

face of a cherub. I quickly realized when we went for a walk on the cliffs that this cherub took nothing for granted."[31] They became good friends and for the next ten years Vernon Watkins was Dylan's constant poetic mentor. Their mutual consultations over poems are recorded in the published letters. Out on the beautiful Pennard Cliffs of Gower where Watkins lived, they read their poems aloud to each other. For a time, when Dylan was preparing his Twenty-Five Poems, they met every Wednesday for lunch at the Kardomah Cafe in Swansea along with Alfred Janes, Tom Warner, the writer John Prichard, and a number of journalists. Dylan listened seriously to Vernon Watkins' advice and accepted suggestions for changes—sometimes:

> I tried to persuade Dylan to leave two of the poems out of the new book of twenty-five. These were the poems beginning "Now, Say Nay . . ." and "How Soon the Servant Sun." The other poems all seemed packed with meaning, but for me these two poems presented a face of unwarrantable obscurity. He himself remarked of one of them that so far as he knew it had no meaning at all. He was, however, firm about including them. When I said that reviewers would be likely to pick these out rather than the fine poems in the book he smiled and said, "Give them a bone."[32]

The book was brought out in September, 1936, by J. M. Dent as the fifteenth volume in the "New Poetry" series. The London Times Literary Supplement said of it:

> Mr. Thomas's language as a poet is so much his own that it is often as difficult to interpret as a foreign tongue. . . . That Mr. Thomas is essentially a poet is certainly proved by the symbolical quality of his language. He writes in images peculiar to himself, but so intensely conceived that it is only when we cease trying to explain them to the reason that we begin to grasp the quality of experience they communicate.[33]

The literary Establishment was rather kinder than his own friend Bernard Spencer who, in his review in New Verse, said that the poems divided themselves into "sense poems" and "nonsense poems." The first he thought good despite their being overliterary, and having images that tended to decorate but not illuminate. The second (and larger) group, he thought, spoke "continually at the top of the voice," were "giddily crammed with images, and trap-doored with private allusions." He felt that the book should be bought because the author had done good poems, but he did not himself find much in it to recommend: "at a time when poetry has a small audience and a great many enemies, it does seem to me that his sort of writing is not only not worth while but harmful. . . ." Such a review was, in part, a reaction against the warmth of those critics who were delighted to find a poet who wrote neither in the style of Eliot nor the style of Auden, and who perhaps overpraised the newest arrival.

At the same time he was being widely reviewed, Dylan was writing his own newspaper reviews—but of quite a different kind. Beginning in 1935, he had written reviews of mystery thrillers, when Grigson was editor of the book pages of the London Morning Post. This fiction, which he enjoyed reading beyond the demands of the job, included works by Mignon Eberhart, John Dickson Carr, Rex Stout, Dorothy Sayers, Erle Stanley Gardner, S. S. Van Dine, Agatha Christie, and Ngaio Marsh. Between September, 1935, and February, 1936, he reviewed some forty-seven of them. A little later, he turned to general fiction, and through December, 1939, reviewed some twenty-eight current novels for the New English Weekly, including titles by Samuel Beckett, William Carlos Williams, J. P. Marquand, Kay Boyle, H. G. Wells, Rose Wilder Lane, John Dos Passos, Franz Kafka, Flann O'Brien, Ruthven Todd, Erskine Caldwell, Frederic Prokosch, and Dorothy Parker.

In the fall of 1937 a man named George Reavey suggested to Dylan that his Europa Press print some sixteen of Dylan's short stories under the title The Burning Baby. Reavey had begun publishing in Paris in 1935 with two books of his own poems and one by Samuel Beckett; his first London edition was The Thorns of Thunder by Paul Eluard in 1936. The contract for The Burning Baby was drawn up and signed in December, 1937, and £20 of advance royalties were paid. The book was announced for June publication along with other books by Samuel Beckett, Paul Eluard, Denis Devlin, and Charles Henri Ford. But Reavey had not reckoned on the sensibilities of the London printers. When they discovered that the title story was a horror-fantasy about a preacher who seduced his daughter, attended the birth of their child, and then burned the baby, they balked. It was this same story that caused Pamela Johnson's mother misgivings when she had typed it a few years earlier; but it had caused no great commotion when Roger Roughton had printed it in the May, 1936, Contemporary Poetry and Prose. In any case the text had to be sent to another set of printers. Augustus John was to do a portrait of Dylan and there was to be a special one-guinea edition

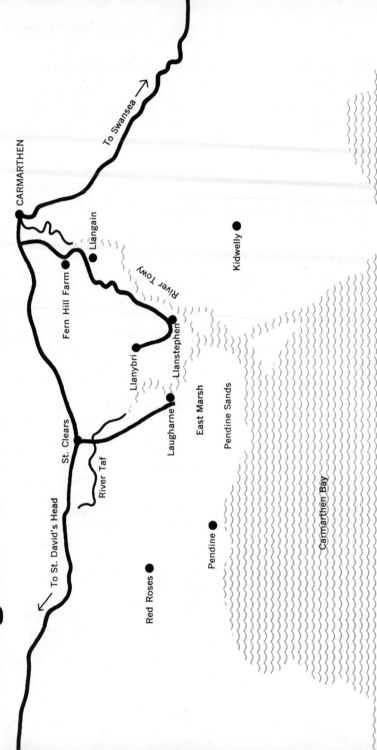

Laugharne and Environs

CARMARTHEN

To Swansea →

Llangain

Fern Hill Farm

River Towy

Kidwelly

Llanybri

Llanstephen

St. Clears

East Marsh

Pendine Sands

Laugharne

River Taf

To St. David's Head

Pendine

Red Roses

Carmarthen Bay

for subscribers. James Laughlin IV, the publisher of New Directions in America, had asked to buy 500 sheets of the edition ("if the writing is very esoteric 300 copies will be enough"); and Henry Miller had written that the Obelisk Press in Paris was keen to get the stories. Reavey even asked Dylan if he could manage the film rights, to which Dylan replied, "How could <u>those</u> stories be filmed? Shirley Temple as the Burning Baby?"

Then troubles began to multiply. John reported that he was unhappy with the portrait and wanted to do another. "Dylan Thomas is an excellent subject but a bad sitter." Dylan was annoyed at the delays: "We may as well wait until the Religious Tract Society offers to publish <u>The Burning Baby</u>." The second set of printers had also found the text too hot to handle; and the publisher had been advised that if he brought out the stories he would be liable to "a large fine and a few months in gaol." Dylan, by now dissatisfied with Reavey, turned the whole matter over to the agent David Higham (of Pearn, Pollinger, and Higham) who was to remain his agent for the rest of his career. By eliminating the controversial "Baby", Higham was able to get Dent to take seven of the stories, which were finally published along with sixteen poems and the John portrait under the title <u>The Map of Love</u> in August, 1939.

Back in December of 1938, the Thomases returned from Sea View to Ringwood to await the arrival of their first child. It was then and for that occasion that Dylan wrote "Poem in the Ninth Month" (later called "A Saint About to Fall"), and also his poem about Cwmdonkin Park, "Once it was the Colour of Saying." Caitlin, in his words, was "very strong and well and full" and so was he. Each day when Caitlin lay down for an afternoon rest, Dylan would do the same, well supplied with soft drinks and his favorite "Dollie Mixture" sweets. At the end of the ninth month, both the prospective mother and father had increased considerably in girth. Caitlin later wrote, "Dylan used to read to me in bed, in our first, know-nothing, lamb-sappy days; to be more exact, Dylan may have been a skinny spring lambkin, but I was more like its buxom mother then, and distinctly recollect carrying him across streams under one arm; till the roles were reversed, and he blew out, and I caved in."[34]

Llewelyn Edouard Thomas was born on January 30, 1939, in the Cornelia Hospital in Poole: "his head is long and fibrous, and his face squashed red and angry like Dylan," Caitlin reported. Her figure returned to normal, but Dylan had lost forever the slim outline of a frail poetic boy. He was now a stocky man, and so he

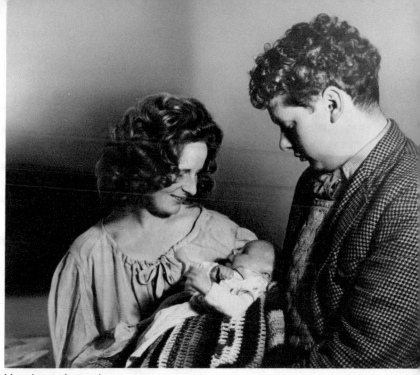

Llewelyn and parents

Dylan by Augustus John

remained. He was, he said, "two stone heavier, but not a feather steadier."

Dylan was not entirely enchanted with the district of the New Forest where they lived. He wrote to Bert Trick in March, 1939, that in this flat, narrow-chested country of fading squires, sour gentlewomen, and professional ostriches, he longed for his old soapbox of bright colors where he could deliver the grand arguments he had learned from the political theories of Trick. He longed for their winter evenings of Cwmdonkin sonnets and the times when they had planned "the annihilation of the ruling classes over sandwiches and jelly and blancmange." Yet Hampshire provided the quiet for the preparation of two books. In December, 1939, The World I Breathe was published by New Directions in America. It was made up of forty poems selected from the first three books published in England, and eleven stories (including the notorious "Baby"), none of which had been published in book form in the United States. Its edition was limited to 700 copies and is now one of the scarcest of the Thomas books. In April of 1940, Portrait of the Artist as a Young Dog was published. Most critics noticed the contrast in style between these stories, so clearly related to James Joyce's autobiographical stories, and the surrealist stories that had come out just the year before in The Map of Love. As the reviewer in Life and Letters Today said, "If Mr. Thomas pursues this clarifying process he will soon be telling a story with all the simple astuteness of Mr. Somerset Maugham."[35]

War Years

The outbreak of war in 1939 had deeply shocked Dylan and at one point he tried to organize a writers' manifesto against war which he hoped would be printed in influential magazines. There was very little response to the idea: Rayner Heppenstall, in fact, suggested that it might even be the writer's duty to undergo contemporary reality at its most extreme. Dylan pounced on this and replied,

> When you come to talk about one's duty as a writer, then one can only say that his duty is to write. If to undergo contemporary reality to its most extreme is to join in a war . . . against people you do not know, and probably to be killed or maimed, then one can only say flippantly that the best poems about death were always written when the poets were alive, that Lorca didn't have to be gored before

writing a bullsong, that for a writer to undergo the utmost reality of poverty is for him to starve to death and therefore to be, as a writer, useless. . . .[36] Bitter about the futility of warfare as a means of solving problems, he said that it was better to "receive a good salary for muddling information, censoring news, licking official stamps, etc., than it is to kill or be killed for a shilling, or less, a day." Later he wrote to Bert Trick that though he had only his feelings to guide him, they were his own, and nothing would turn him savage against people with whom he had no quarrel. He said there was a need now for some life to go on strenuously and patiently outside the dictated hates and pettiness of war and that life, he, for his part, intended to continue to support by writing and thinking and living as coolly, hotly, and as well as he knew how.

Finally, he decided to declare himself a conscientious objector. He went up to the tribunal in North Wales where he was preceded by a series of fundamentalist objectors. As each was interrogated and asked the grounds of his objection, each tight-lipped, righteous, chapel-going Welshman murmured "—ligious." Observing the lot, Dylan knew that his place was not among them. He could not say that his grounds were theirs.

In late April of 1940 Dylan got the announcement that he was to be called up for service. At the same time panic set in over another matter. Deep in debt, he had to raise £70 to save his and Caitlin's possessions from being seized and themselves from being turned out of their house. Desperate, he explained his difficulty to Stephen Spender, who said that he would try to raise a fund for him. With the cooperation of Peter Watson, Henry Moore, and Herbert Read, Spender prepared an appeal which was mailed to literary men— J. B. Priestley, Hugh Walpole, H. G. Wells, Richard Hughes, Richard Llewelyn, Cecil Day Lewis, Louis Golding, and many others. Money came in very quickly and soon more than the required amount was available. But since Dylan's inexpertness in handling money was well known, a number of the subscribers to the fund suggested that the fund-raisers should see that the money actually got to the creditors, and Spender asked Dylan to send the bills directly to him for payment. When this was done, the remainder of the fund, some twelve or thirteen pounds, was sent on to Dylan, who gratefully acknowledged that everything was in good order. He then thought that he might join the Royal Army Medical Corps; he would register, as he put it, as "a never-fighter." When he was finally called up for his physical examination in Llanelly, he had been preparing for it for some time by increasingly stiff drinking sessions. Arriving in front of the medical examiners with a monumental hangover, he was genuinely sick on the spot, and was, in the end, diagnosed as an acute asthmatic and put down at the very bottom of the list of those suitable for fighting.

Thus, in the spring of 1940, although Dylan was freed of war-service responsibilities, his circumstances were still not very happy—he not only did not have a satisfactory source of income, he was also "without a penny and hopelessly in debt" in Ringwood and Laugharne.

The Malting House

Temporary relief came in the form of an invitation to the Thomases from John Davenport and his wife to join them in the Cotswolds at a place called the Malting House, where a number of writers, artists, and musicians were in residence. There Dylan went with Caitlin and the infant Llewelyn to live from June, 1940, to the following January in the big house in Marshfield near Chippenham, Wiltshire, with Humphrey Searle, Henry Boys, Lennox Berkeley, Arnold Cooke, Antonia White, William Glock, and others. There he collaborated with John Davenport in writing alternate chapters of a detective story, Death of the King's Canary. The original idea for such a novel had been Pamela Hansford Johnson's. It was to be about an imaginary poet laureate and, referring to the laureate's emolument, to be called No More Canary Wine. The title was changed, and the final work couldn't be published because it was considered libelous on a number of well-known people who were portrayed not with entire kindness. It deals with the death of a poet laureate and the problems surrounding the choice of his successor. Every conceivable candidate refuses the post, until the drink-loving anarchist, being attracted by the emolument of a butt of Malmsey, accepts. All the leading literary figures of the day are invited to a banquet of celebration. As Vernon Watkins describes it, parodies of their works are read at the banquet, which becomes an increasingly embarrassing mixture of squalor, fake courtesy, and confusion. The guests, many of them contemporary writers in more or less affectionate caricature, behave according to their dignity or lack of it. A part of the book—Dylan's parody of his friend William Empson—did appear in Horizon (July, 1942).

On an occasion when he was upset at not receiving two pounds which Vernon Watkins had sent him, Dylan wrote from the Malting House: "Mad things have been happening to letters: I've lost one before, about three weeks ago. I think this house must be marked, and the letters opened. Really. The house, as I told you is full of musicians, all are young men, not one is in the army, one has a German name, there was a German staying here some time ago, and there have also been five lighting offences in about six weeks."[37]

The spring publication of Portrait of the Artist as a Young Dog had increased his reputation so that by late summer of 1940 he had acquired a job with the BBC preparing scripts to be translated into Portuguese and broadcast to Brazil. "I've got an exciting one to do next, on Columbus," he wrote. "But I haven't settled down to a poem for a long time. I want to, and will soon, but it mustn't be nightmarish."[38] Poems were beginning to come more and more slowly.

Documentary Films

On one of his trips to London from the Malting House, Dylan had run into Ivan Moffat, an apprentice screen writer and the son of Iris Tree and the expatriate American painter Curtis Moffat. He introduced Dylan to his employer Donald Taylor, presenting him rather melodramatically as being rejected by the Army, suffering from advanced consumption, and starving. Taylor, who already knew Dylan's work through Twenty-Five Poems, took instantly to the man at their meeting on a fine summer evening, and Dylan took to him. A friendship and a close working relationship that was to continue for the next four years was begun when Dylan accepted a position with Taylor's company, Strand Films of Golden Square, and became a trainee writer for documentary films.

The thirties and forties marked the efflorescence of the British documentary film movement. John Grierson and Basil Wright had produced The Country Comes to the Town in 1931; Grierson announced his "first principles of documentary making" in 1932; and Wright produced the great Song of Ceylon in 1934. Donald Taylor had learned his trade from the Empire Market Board Film Unit and the G.P.O. Film Unit under John Grierson, who was chiefly concerned to use films as a purely educational and sociological instrument. Taylor was interested in introducing documentary techniques into the commercial world and therefore left Grierson to create his own firm. He was joined by Paul Rotha, with whom Taylor had worked on abstract films in the G.P.O. unit, and Ralph Keene, a former director of Tooth's Art Gallery. To get away from the conventional "film writers," the new firm adopted a deliberate policy of employing good writers but not necessarily men with film experience. Graham Greene was one of the first to work for them, Philip Lindsay was another, and Taylor was delighted to "discover" Dylan Thomas.

Dylan was immediately put to work on a series of films as script writer and adapter, working, as is customary in the profession, with a team of writers. Consequently not much of his documentary work can be isolated for examination. This is Colour, for example, a five-minute film made for the Imperial Chemical Industries, despite its brevity, employed five writers of whom Dylan was one. Dylan, again, was but one of six writers on the film C.E.M.A. (Council for the Encouragement of Music and Art) made for the Ministry of Information.

During this film-making period the Thomases lived in various places. For a while there was Chelsea—a tumbledown studio full of cats on Manresa Road, and then a basement apartment on Markham Square. For short periods they used John Davenport's Rossetti House on Flood Street. Often he would take his work with him to the country so that from January through April, 1941, they were with Dylan's parents in Bishopston, and from May through August with Richard Hughes in Laugharne.

There are several documentaries, five- or twelve-minute films, which Dylan did nearly or entirely alone: New Towns for Old (June, 1942); Balloon Site 568, with Ivan Moffat (July, 1942); Wales (December, 1942); These Are The Men, with Alan Osbiston (March, 1943); and—most notably—Our Country, a fifty-minute film made in 1944. This, the longest documentary on which Dylan worked, aroused a great deal of discussion in the film world. The Documentary News Letter printed three different discussions of the picture and included a full page of excerpts from the poetic commentary. This lyrical look at the face of wartime Britain was largely creditable to its director John Eldridge, with a strong assist from his poet-writer and his composer, William Alwyn. The News Letter called it "the sole and successful experimental film of the war period." The picture presented a lyrical, impressionistic view of Britain in which a merchant sailor traveled about from the ships of Liverpool through the airfields of Kent and the mining valleys of South Wales, finally to the lumber camps of Scotland. A propaganda film, it documented the Britisher with insight and affection, and in the script were included brief lyrics on such subjects as felling trees, St. Paul's, Glasgow, Aberdeen and London. It did not win unqualified approval; some critics considered the poetic commentary superfluous; but most of them found it important and

"I walked abroad in a shower of all my days"

Baby Aeron and parents

good. It was in Dylan's characteristic style, as when a train starts up:

> Going out
> out over the racing rails in a grumble of London-
> leaving thunder
> over the maze track of metal
> through a wink and a spin of towns and signals
> and fields
> out
> to the edges of the explosive the moon-moved man-
> indifferent capsizing sea.[39]

One of Dylan's films never got released because of its irreverence. Taking off from a poster, issued by the government during the war, that was intended to keep people from making excessive use of the transportation facilities and which read IS YOUR JOURNEY REALLY NECESSARY?, the well-known comedy director Oswald Mitchell and Dylan produced a parody entitled Is Your Ernie Really Necessary? The resourceful actor Haypetrie played all the parts. In one scene, Haypetrie, as a railroad signalman, played "The Bells of St. Mary's" on the signal levers. In another scene he was dressed as a chorus girl, reflected by optical process twelve times so that he looked like a chorus line. The horrified Ministry of Information rejected the film instanter.

Dylan's regular work with Donald Taylor's Strand Films stood him in good stead, for on March 3, 1943, his family was increased to four when a daughter, Aeron, was born in London. At the height of its operations the film company was producing around seventy-five films a year, developing ideas for industry and for government, and then producing the films under contract. Since this was one of the most intense periods of World War II, most of the work was propaganda done on commission for the Office of War Information.

At the end of 1943 Taylor closed out the Strand operation, and, with a reduced staff, formed a new company, Gryphon Films, for which Dylan worked through 1944. With the idea of producing feature films, Taylor commissioned Dylan to do a Life of Robert Burns, based on Catherine Carswell's biography (the scenario is now lost); The Doctor and the Devils, which has since been presented in a stage adaptation, and Twenty Years A-Growing, based on Maurice O'Sullivan's idyllic account of a boy's life in the Blasket Islands off the coast of Kerry. None of these feature films was produced.

Dylan, who loved being a chameleon and adapting

himself to any situation or playing any role, greatly enjoyed the company of film people. Frequently, Donald Taylor recalls, they would decide beforehand what role they both were going to play when they went out for a drink; this may explain the somewhat contradictory recollections of Dylan. His favorite role was that of a Welsh country gentleman, for which he dressed in hairy tweeds, carried a knobbed walking stick, and used his very good "posh" accent. Alternatively he would be the BBC actor and verse reader, for which he wore a light gray smooth-tweed suit. Being the drunken Welsh poet with "fag in the corner of the mouth, and dirty raincoat, and polo sweater" sometimes lasted for a week or more. The Gargoyle Club, where he sometimes worked on scripts, saw a whole succession of Dylans.

A sensational episode occurred in March, 1945. The Thomases were then living in Cardiganshire in the Welsh town of New Quay, which perches precariously on a cliffside above the sea. It was this town that provided the background for the radio talk "Quite Early One Morning," a precursor of Under Milk Wood. Donald Taylor, having despaired of getting Dylan to settle down on his own to a script, had sent the prospective director John Eldridge and secretary Fanya Fisher down to New Quay to work with him. One evening when the three were together in a pub, a young paratrooper captain made some anti-Semitic remarks to Miss Fisher: she attacked him, scoring both his cheeks with her nails. When the friends left the pub for the Black Lion Hotel, they were followed by the captain, who struck Miss Fisher on the face. Dylan, going to her assistance, got involved in a fist fight with the paratrooper. Later that night, when Dylan had returned to the Majoda Bungalow in New Quay where he was staying with his family, he and his guests were suddenly alarmed to hear gunfire at the back of the house; the next moment there were bullets flying around the living room. The door burst open and the captain came in, wearing dark glasses, his face bloody, carrying a Sten submachine gun in one hand and a hand grenade in the other. He fired the machine gun into the ceiling. Dylan somehow managed to get it away from him, but then he would not leave, he said, until the gun was returned to him, and threatened to throw the grenade and blow them all up. He was finally persuaded to leave peaceably. Several months later, he was charged with being illegally in possession of firearms and of shooting with intent to murder. By that time tempers had cooled and the jury acquitted him.

But life, generally, during the several months in New Quay was not unpleasant; as he wrote to a friend: "It is very lovely here; I have a shack at the edge of the cliff where my children hop like

"With water praying and call of seagull and rook"

fleas in a box—in London, the only remaining flea-circus I have seen is pushed about the streets in one half of a child's pram—and my wife grumbles at me and them and the sea for the mess we all make, and I work among cries and clatters like a venomous beaver in a parrot house."[40]

Dylan had begun his work for Taylor at ten pounds a week; by the time he left he was getting twenty—a not inconsiderable sum for a staff writer in those days. Caitlin Thomas sometimes claimed the weekly paycheck had destroyed Dylan's poetic capacity, that the sense of security militated against his lyrical gifts. But the truth is that Dylan's native anarchism was always at odds with an enormous desire for a regular income. Later on, the absence of money merely led to deeper despair—not to the production of more poems. It was, in fact, during 1944, while he was working for Donald Taylor, that he completed what has become one of his most popular works, the second of two poems called "Poem in October." It had apparently been conceived in Laugharne when he and Caitlin were living in Sea View. One of his own favorite poems, it has been translated into many languages. It is particularly interesting to anyone concerned with versification because it reveals, better than any other single poem, Dylan's method of regularizing the length of line, not by the use of traditional meter but by a fixed number of syllables for each line.[41] In this poem, each stanza has ten lines, with the lines following the pattern of 9 syllables, then 12, 9, 3, 5, 12, 12, 5, 3, and 9.

Poem in October

It was my thirtieth year to heaven
Woke to my hearing from harbour and neighbour wood
And the mussel pooled and the heron
Priested shore
The morning beckon
With water praying and call of seagull and rook
And the knock of sailing boats on the net webbed wall
Myself to set foot
That second
In the still sleeping town and set forth.

My birthday began with the water-
Birds and the birds of the winged trees flying my name
Above the farms and the white horses
And I rose
In rainy autumn
And walked abroad in a shower of all my days.
High tide and the heron dived when I took the road
Over the border
And the gates
Of the town closed as the town awoke.

A springful of larks in a rolling
Cloud and the roadside bushes brimming with whistling
Blackbirds and the sun of October
Summery
On the hill's shoulder,
Here were fond climates and sweet singers suddenly
Come in the morning where I wandered and listened
To the rain wringing
Wind blow cold
In the wood faraway under me.

Pale rain over the dwindling harbour
And over the sea wet church the size of a snail
With its horns through mist and the castle
Brown as owls
But all the gardens
Of spring and summer were blooming in the tall tales
Beyond the border and under the lark full cloud.
There could I marvel
My birthday
Away but the weather turned around.

It turned away from the blithe country
And down the other air and the blue altered sky
Streamed again a wonder of summer
With apples
Pears and red currants
And I saw in the turning so clearly a child's
Forgotten mornings when he walked with his mother
Through the parables
Of sun light
And the legends of the green chapels

And the twice told fields of infancy
That his tears burned my cheeks and his heart moved in mine.
These were the woods the river and sea
Where a boy
In the listening
Summertime of the dead whispered the truth of his joy
To the trees and the stones and the fish in the tide.
And the mystery
Sang alive
Still in the water and singingbirds.

And there could I marvel my birthday
Away but the weather turned around. And the true
Joy of the long dead child sang burning
In the sun.
It was my thirtieth
Year to heaven stood there then in the summer noon
Though the town below lay leaved with October blood.
O may my heart's truth
Still be sung
On this high hill in a year's turning.

"On the hill's shoulder . . . the wood faraway under me"

Craftsmanship

Few writers have shown the meticulous care for craftsmanship that marked Dylan Thomas' practice. Working slowly and with infinite pains, he would experiment with a single phrase, writing it a hundred different ways before he was content. Often he used a separate worksheet for each line of a poem, sometimes pages of trials for a single line as the poem was gradually built up. One line might occupy him for days. He usually had an idea of a poem's eventual length before he began, and would then decide how many lines to give to each of its sections. After the whole first draft had been completed, the real work began. Every time a change was made in the text, he would recopy the entire poem by hand and begin again. He disliked typewriters and got other people to type copies when it was necessary. As he wrote to Pamela Hansford Johnson, typing makes the warmest words look cold. His technical complexity is illustrated in "I, in my Intricate Image," a poem which includes seventy-two variations on the letter L in the line endings, twenty-four in each of the three parts.

Perhaps the most remarkable example of his craftsmanship is in the rhyming of the introduction to his Collected Poems; the rhyme scheme of the first half of the 102-line poem mirrors the second half: the first and last lines of the poem rhyme; the second and the last but one; and so on. Fond as he was of beer, he never was other than clear-headed when he sat down in the afternoon, his favorite time for work. Then he made experiment after experiment with sound, rhythm, and idea, piling the floor high with rolled-up discarded versions in his careful handwriting, until finally, after days and weeks and, in many cases, years of consideration, he released a poem for publication.

As work for Donald Taylor decreased in 1945, there was a period of increased poetic productivity, when Dylan was writing the poems which were to appear in Deaths and Entrances, published on February 7, 1946. This book increased his reputation considerably. It led to such an estimate of his works as that of Denis Botterill in Life and Letters:

> It is a rare occurrence for the early supporters of a new poet to be so triumphantly vindicated as those who courageously backed Dylan Thomas more than a decade ago. The promise of those early years has now produced a poet of such stature that it

With Patric Dickinson, head of BBC poetry programs, 1946

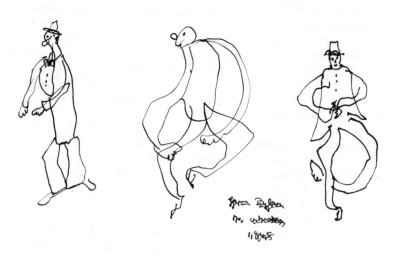

Dylan doodles

> becomes difficult to assess him without new
> apparatus and a lengthy search for poetical
> antecedents. . . . The poetry of Dylan Thomas surges
> up from the wellspring of his being with a power
> and an abandon which would seem reckless were it
> not controlled by a splendid craftsmanship which
> never falters or betrays the author into rhetoric,
> bombast, or bathos.[42]

Life was good in the summer and fall of 1946. The war was
over, and though the austerities were to continue, there was a
fine respite for the Thomas family on a vacation jaunt to Dublin and
Kerry. "We ate ourself daft: lobsters, steaks, cream, hills of butter,
homemade bread, chicken and chocolates: we drank Seithenyns of
porter and Guinness: we walked, climbed, rode on donkeys, bathed,
sailed, rowed, danced, sang."[43] And in November Dylan's Selected
Writings, the contents of which he had chosen himself, were brought
out by James Laughlin and prepared the way for his fame in America.

Radio Work

After he had worked for several years as a staff script writer
preparing documentary films and writing unproduced features, Dylan
became active with the BBC. Two of his poems ("Light" and the
first "Poem in October") had been printed in The Listener as early as
March and October, 1934. And his first broadcast, "Life and the
Modern Poet," was given in Swansea on April 21, 1937. From then to
the end of his life he was a frequent contributor to radio programs
and a frequent performer as well. In the three years beginning in
October, 1945, he did over a hundred broadcasts, mostly for the
series called Book of Verse produced by John Arlott for the Overseas
Service. Arlott says:

> I worked with him some twenty or thirty times a
> year from 1945 to 1950, on literary programmes of
> every type. He was always open-minded to
> experiment; in his own word "easy"; while his
> immense depth of reading in poetry—which he never
> paraded—and his very real integrity made him
> the perfect touchstone for a producer. The
> weight he gave to each word, idea, and line in
> his reading demanded strength of thought and
> structure in a poem and once, exclaiming
> against the arrogance of a piece by Coventry

Patmore, he said, "Please don't ask me to read it: I hate it too much." When an extract from a poem by Sir Lewis Morris was included in a programme, Dylan doubted that he ought to attempt to read it, and thought it might be better "thrown away" by a lighter reader. He agreed to try it, however, and on first reading, fell into a fairly strong Welsh accent which lifted the poem higher than we had thought possible, for Morris, also a Welshman, had written it in a pattern of Welsh speech rhythms not apparent to the reading eye.

In a programme on Doughty, he had to read a piece from "The Dawn in Britain" in which occurred a word whose meaning the producer, script-writer and reader all admitted they did not know, although it appeared to be the key-word of an essential passage. Our sources of reference could not help and we pondered the problem at some length until Dylan said comfortingly, "Never mind, I'll say it with conviction."[44]

Of the many people with whom he worked at the BBC—Patric Dickinson, Aneirin Davies, Roy Campbell, Louis MacNeice— Dylan held Louis MacNeice in his closest affection. The Irishman was a congenial drinking companion as well as an expert and knowledgeable poet whose advice Dylan cherished. When MacNeice adapted "Trimalchio's Feast" from Petronius' Satyricon for radio performance, Dylan was one of the actors. (He had also taken the leading role in Aeschylus' Agamemnon, in several Shakespearean productions, and the role of Satan in an adaptation of Paradise Lost.) Speaking as a radio producer, MacNeice has described Dylan's radio acting:

He was . . . a subtle and versatile actor, as he proved repeatedly in radio performances. And he "took production." Though his special leaning (as was natural, given his astonishing voice) was to the sonorous and emotional, he enjoyed playing character parts, especially comic or grotesque ones, such as a friendly Raven which he played for me once in a dramatised Norwegian folk-tale. He could even "throw away" if required to. And in all these sidelines—as in all his verse and prose— there appeared the same characteristic blend of

delight in what he was doing and care as to how
he did it.[45]

When the BBC Third Programme was started, Roy Campbell was
put in charge of literature, and he found many opportunities to
make use of Dylan:

Dylan was [Campbell said] the best all-round
reader of verse I ever produced, though John
Lawrie ran him close, and an Irishman called
Hutchinson. Dylan only had one weakness—he
could not read correct poets like Pope or Dryden. He
was best at the "wild and woolly" poets. I used to
keep him on beer all day till he had done his night's
work and then take him down to the duty room
where the charming Miss Backhouse or Miss Tofield
would pour us both a treble whisky as a reward for
our labours. It was with Blake and Manley Hopkins
that Dylan became almost Superman: but we had
bad luck with Dryden. Dylan had got at the whisky
first and he started behaving like a prima donna. He
insisted on having an announcer instead of
beginning the programme right away as we used to
on the Third Programme. There were only two
minutes to go and I rushed back to the studio and
found Dylan snoring in front of the mike with only
twenty seconds left. He was slumped back in his
chair, with an almost seraphic expression of blissful
peace. I shook him awake, and, to his horror and
consternation, began announcing him, not in my
South African accent, but trying to talk like an
English announcer, with my tonsils, in an "Oxford
accent." Dylan nearly jumped out of his skin with
fright and horror: and was almost sober when he got
the green light, though he did bungle the title as
"Ode on Shaint Sheshilia's Day"; but after that his
voice cleared up and I began to breathe again. When
he had finished reading the "Ode" I got another
fright: he began to beckon me wildly with his arms
and point to the page before him. I got the engineer
to switch off the mike and slipped into the studio
again. Dylan had forgotten how to pronounce
"Religio Laici." I told him and slipped out. He had
about three shots at it, bungled it, gave it up; and

Poetry reading on the Third Programme

Vernon Watkins, John Prichard, Fred Janes, John Griffiths,
Dan Jones, Dylan Thomas, Oct. 24, 1949

then went on reading. The next day I was hauled up in front of George Barnes, but he was a good boss and had a sense of humour. I promised to keep an eye on Dylan: Dylan promised to keep an eye on himself—and he kept his word. I used him for several readings, a wonderful performance that he gave of Cervantes' Two Dogs, and many other poetry readings: and his performance was flawless from then on.[46]

Most of Dylan's original contributions to broadcasting were created for the Welsh Home Service, and some of the most successful of these are the autobiographical reports "Memories of Christmas" and "Return Journey." The first, prepared for the holiday season of 1945, was later added to a newspaper piece "Conversation about Christmas" to compose the now-famous A Child's Christmas in Wales. The most popular of all his radio pieces was undoubtedly "Return Journey," the story of his visit to Swansea after the war. In this he tells of the devastation the three-night blitz of February, 1941, wrought on the center of Swansea and poignantly recalls himself, first as a reporter, then as a schoolboy, and finally as a child. Eight of these autobiographical essays-for-radio, along with other more formal pieces of literary criticism and reportage, have been edited by Aneirin Talfan Davies, director of the BBC Welsh Region, under the title Quite Early One Morning (1954).

Bohemianism

There was always conflict in Dylan between self-indulgent bohemianism and the responsibilities and proprieties of a family man. As he once wrote, "I have been in London, in penury, and in doubt: In London, because money lives and breeds there; in penury, because it doesn't; and in doubt as to whether I should continue as an outlaw or take my fate for a walk in the straight and bowler-treed paths. The conceit of outlaws is a wonderful thing; they think they can join the ranks of regularly-conducted society whenever they like."[47] He was making a good income in 1946, as he was to do for the rest of his life, but the couple's improvidence was such that no matter what sums came to hand there was never enough left to pay for the basic necessities. These two sides of his character are revealed in two pictures: the photograph of the solid citizen of the noble BBC Third Programme, leaning against a reliable column; and

The Mandrake Club, Soho

Dylan by Michael Ayrton

The Savage Club, Carleton House Terrace

"The ranks of regularly conducted society"

the drawing by Michael Ayrton which shows him as the eternally
disheveled child. The division in his temperament is also symbolized
by the two clubs he frequented most: The Savage Club on Carlton
House Terrace was comparatively genteel, frequented by writers and
artists like John Davenport, the Welsh operatic tenor Parry Jones, and
the writer Norman Cameron, each of whom sponsored his membership
there. Before joining the Savage in 1949, Dylan had frequented the
even more respectable National-Liberal Club on Whitehall Place.
He once wrote to Pamela Johnson that she alone knew how True-Blue
he really was, and what a collection of old school ties his vest
concealed. The Mandrake Club, however, another favorite resort, was a
down-at-the-heels joint off Dean Street in the midst of Soho dives
which almost anyone who had the small fee could join. While most
people had no hint of it, Caitlin was acutely aware of many of his
curiously bourgeois preferences:

> . . . Though Dylan imagined himself to be
> completely emancipated from his family background
> [she wrote], there was a very strong puritanical
> streak in him, that his friends never suspected; but
> of which I got the disapproving benefit. Those who
> only saw his bar-leaning, on, and on, and on story,
> with no detectable end, telling; would never credit
> that other punctilious, pettifogging niggler for detail,
> making such a fuss over the correct dress for me
> to wear for the . . . market, I mean it, right down to
> gloves, stockings, shoes; and he would have
> preferred a hat, but knew that was too much, even
> for him, to ask of me. . . .
>
> Dylan and I fell between the two extremes; and
> though we both had a great loathing for poverty and
> squalor and did all we could, which was mostly talk,
> to get out of it, and achieve that ideal state of
> bourgeois respectability and armchair comfort we
> both craved; or to be exact, Dylan did; to me there
> was nothing between the barn and the Salon; we
> never quite, though we got pretty near, achieved it.
> It was the same thing with money: we spent hours
> planning all the sensible, civilized things we would
> do with it; eking it out on moderate enjoyment, like
> proper people; vowing and swearing before our
> Holy Maker, never again to indulge in those racketing
> wastes that wrought such havoc in us; and in which

a good half of our lives was spent. But the valuable
quality of moderation was totally lacking in both of
us; in one was bad enough, but in both it was fatal.[48]

The wild aspect of Caitlin's character is revealed in detail in her book
from which the quotation comes, Leftover Life to Kill. Neither
Dylan nor Caitlin was capable of the dull life of the bon bourgeois,
no matter how much they may have longed for it.

In Italy

The spring of 1947 was a time of excitement. The whole family, plus
Caitlin's sister Brigit Marnier and her two-year-old son Tobias, were
to go to Italy. With the help of friends, they had been able to obtain
the use of a beautiful hillside house with a grandly colonnaded
swimming pool, the Villa di Beccaro at Mosciano in the Florentine
suburb of Sandicci. In the first week of April the party of three adults
and three children set out. They stopped in Santa Margherita on
the Italian Riviera for three weeks, and then moved on to Florence.

There Dylan had immediate entrée to the Florentine
literati, for Luigi Berti had just published in his Inventario some
Italian translations of his poems. Thanks to Berti, and as a result of
favorable critical notices in Boccaporto and Boccaporto Secondo,
Dylan became acquainted with Mario Luzi, Piero Bigongiari, Eugenio
Montale, Alessandro Parronchi, the painter Ottone Rosai, and other
artists and writers. Unfortunately, the language barrier prevented
any real communication: none of the English knew Italian, and few of
the Italians knew English. Dylan and the two women felt isolated
and lonely. There was, of course, the sunny climate and the élan of
the Florentines to make the first two months exciting. But this was not
enough to last. "We have got to know lots of the young intellectuals
of Florence," Dylan wrote to a friend, "and a damp lot they are.
They visit us on Sundays. To overcome the language, I have to stand
on my head, fall in the pool, crack nuts with my teeth, and Tarzan in
the cypresses. I am very witty in Italian, though a little violent;
and I need space. Do you know anybody in Florence nice to have a
drink with?"[49]

The reference to the tree and the pool were not
fanciful. There were celebrations when more than two guests arrived
at the beautiful villa, and at least one of the parties ended with
everyone jumping fully dressed into the swimming pool. At first Dylan
did not drink wine and, as he wrote to the same friend, "What a
sun-pissed pig I am not to dip a bristle in Chianti. A few days ago I

climbed a tree, forgetting my shape and weight."

The only Englishman of note in Florence at this time
was Stephen Spender. But the difference between the two personalities
seemed too great to permit their being close friends. Dylan was not
interested in intellectual pursuits, and preferred to seek out the places
where the wine and beer were best. He liked the little stand-up wine
bars and the cafes. One of these was the open-air Cafe Giubbe Rosse,
a gathering place of writers and artists in the heart of Florence,
where he was frequently to be found, friendly enough, offering those
who approached a drink but because of the language barrier
remaining largely silent.

The eagerly anticipated stay in Florence was, on the
whole, a gloomy one. But there were moments of brightness such
as the day Dylan organized a country outing and the whole household
of six piled into a horse-drawn cart and drove merrily through the
Tuscan hills. There were periods of social harmony, too—but these
moments were the exception. Dylan was clearly not a happy man
in Florence. Mario Luzi has described his actions:

> One evening, expected to supper with the poet
> Montale, he was reluctantly dragged from his bed
> and remained drunk all the evening. Invited on other
> occasions to their houses by his translator Bigongiari
> and Rosai, the painter, he seemed at first to enter
> into the conversation, a glow of fiery youth in his
> eyes, but almost at once fell back in his chair and
> slept heavily.
>
> And yet, in spite of his drunkenness, his
> reluctance or inability to speak, his myth remains.
> These things merged into an impression of
> incommunicability which, strange though it may
> seem, roused sympathetic liking and commanded
> respect. Those who knew little or nothing of him
> clearly recognized that destiny or a fatal play of
> natural forces was at work within him. Moreover, he
> felt and repaid as best he could the sympathy which
> surrounded him, as for example when, at a lively
> gathering in the house of Parronchi, he suddenly
> became animated, reading aloud from Milton and
> Shakespeare, giving a melodious, profound and
> extraordinarily vigorous rendering, which left a deep
> impression as of a discovery of the old texts and
> of the reader.[50]

The fact is that Dylan was homesick for his own people. Regularly, he would shut himself up and work. It was in this lovely hillside villa, looking out over the spring-green Tuscan hills, that he finished the poem "In Country Sleep"—the one that begins as a lullaby to his daughter and ends as a prophecy: "And you shall wake, from country sleep, this dawn and each first dawn, / Your faith as deathless as the outcry of the ruled sun." But this was the only poem that the stay produced. With no great reluctance the group pulled up stakes and in August moved to Elba.

There Dylan was happier. He liked the people of Elba. The family went to the beach daily and lived in and by the water. Dylan, according to a probably apocryphal report, used to take books with him out onto a rock in the harbor and, when he had absorbed and digested what he needed, threw the books into the water. The writer Augusto Livi affectionately recalls these Elban days when the English group and the Elbans shared a mutual admiration: "And so this year in the village of high houses and stone steps even the little red dogs used to stop at the corners of the steep streets where the poet Dylan Thomas would pass with his head of a Bacchus and his two-toned clothing, his trousers green and his shirt pink."[51]

But sadly, the self-destructiveness that had begun during his first year in London had increased gradually as, approaching middle age, Dylan became more and more acutely aware that his emotional and intellectual resources were being strained. The gloom of the Italian journey was but the first of increasingly frequent periods of despair. Money helped for short periods, but drink soon became the only regular remedy. And from now to the end of his life this recourse was to become more frequent.

In Oxfordshire

On their return from Italy, the Thomases through the generosity of Margaret Taylor settled in Oxfordshire. Dylan had known historian A. J. P. Taylor and his wife Margaret as early as 1935 when he spent a month with them near Manchester. Early in the war years, Dylan and Caitlin spent a Christmas with them in Oxford, and saw them occasionally after that. In September of 1946 the Thomases turned up at the Taylors' in desperate straits: Dylan had broken his arm and they had been turned out of their Chelsea flat. The Taylors took them in and they spent the following winter in the garden cottage of Holywell Ford, Magdalen College. When the cottage proved too crowded, Mrs. Taylor, who was extremely fond of Dylan, obtained a

Dylan

The Boat House on the Taf Estuary, Laugharne

trailer that he might have a studio. In September, 1947, she bought a tumbledown old place in South Leigh, Oxfordshire, called the Manor House, a damp and sagging structure with no hot water or even a bath. This was the house to which all the Thomases, including Dylan's parents, moved, and there they lived until March, 1949.

Feature Films

In addition to writing poems and doing radio work, while living in South Leigh Dylan had begun to work on films again. Ralph Keene, with whom Dylan had earlier worked on documentary films, had now gone on to J. Arthur Rank's Gainsborough Films at the Lime Grove Studios. There Keene suggested to his executive producer that Dylan would be an excellent addition to his staff. Thus it came about that Sydney Box placed Dylan under contract to produce three scripts during 1948. The first was Rebecca's Daughters, an historical piece about the hooded raiders from Wales; the second was The Beach of Falesá, based on the Robert Louis Stevenson short story; and the third was a film operetta, Me and My Bike. Jan Read, scenario editor for Mr. Box, who was in charge of Dylan's work, did not find his job easy:

> [Dylan's] habit was to spend every penny of any advance before beginning work and there would be desperate messages, begging for further advances to pay the tradesmen or buy Christmas presents for the children, so that scripting could continue. Writers ourselves in the scenario department, we did our best for him; but he remained the wonder and despair of the studio accountants. When he did get down to the script he wrote at great speed; and there is a story . . . that, months behind on a previous subject, he asked to be locked into a hotel bedroom with a case of whiskey and finished both the script and the whiskey over the weekend. As a person I found him charming and without side or pretensions. He was unpunctual, it is true, to the extent of turning up for a script meeting a day or two late— generally with some disarming excuse as that he had only a few minutes ago phoned his agent to inquire the date. When he did arrive at Lime Grove, it was always in a rumpled blue serge suit, looking

> like a merchant seaman on shore leave. There was
> never much work done on these occasions; instead,
> we inevitably adjourned to the Shepherd's Bush
> Hotel to down pints of beer and listen to his Welsh
> stories, which he told beautifully. . . . Thomas was
> not the man to bother overmuch with technical
> requirements. Most of the points agreed in
> discussion he used to forget in Soho pubs long
> before returning to Oxford and work.[52]

Unfortunately the film industry underwent a recession in 1948 and
Rank decided to sell the studio before any of the three films were
put into production.

Even before joining the Rank organization Dylan had
done some nondocumentary work. After leaving Gryphon Films in
1944, he was a staff writer for the Stratford Film Company and
worked with a group of writers in producing the scripts for No Room
at the Inn and Three Weird Sisters. Although his individual
contributions to these two films cannot be traced, certain of his
countrymen held his part in the second of these against him, for,
dealing with Welsh materials, it describes the Welshman as having "a
lie in his teeth and a hymn on his lips." Later, in 1950, Dylan was
commissioned to make an adaptation of Vanity Fair, but the project
never got beyond the idea stage. And in 1952 (although funds were
never found for it) Michael Powell had Dylan's agreement to write a
short film, a kind of masque, of a scene from the Odyssey, which was
to be accompanied by two or three arias and instrumental music
composed by Igor Stravinsky.

Since working in London was never congenial to
Dylan, he would, as often as possible, take his assignments home.
After the necessary first conference, he would drop in at the Savage
Club for a final drink, then call for his driver friend Bert Newlands,
pile into the back of the car (to fall asleep on the floor with his feet on
the seat) and head for South Leigh. In the sleepy country town,
life was better. Still there was never enough money. As he wrote to
his fellow BBC worker and godmother to his daughter Aeron, the
composer Elisabeth Lutyens, "It is pauper week in the Old Manor, and
the bills are wailing. Next week, who knows? I may have gold boots.
I haven't been in London much, am trying to write a poem about
Heaven. I am supposed to be writing the script of a musical called
'Me and the Bike,' but haven't got down to it yet. Our dog is horribly
well. I'm going to Edinburgh next week to read poems at the Festival.
My own poem is grand, purple, sonorous, odd."[53] In a house isolated

in the mist of a large foggy meadow, family life went its intense, colorful way. With a household of six souls to care for, with no electricity and only cold water in the kitchen, Caitlin's duties were staggering. For a time Dylan's mother was bedridden with a fractured hip and his father needed constant attention because of a weak heart. But Caitlin contained within herself a whole staff of servants, cooks, and nurses—shampooing and setting Florrie Thomas' hair, looking after the fragile old gentleman working his Times crossword puzzle by the fire, repairing clothes for Llewelyn, untangling Aeron's golden curls, and even bathing Dylan in a Victorian hip-bath.

Both Dylan and Caitlin loved to dress up. Even when they were only going to the Mason Arms to have a drink with the innkeeper, Mrs. Hopkins, they would often be dressed to kill—Dylan in a large tweed sports coat, a check cap set straight on his head, muffler, and gloves—or sometimes in an outfit of hairy velour—plus Wellington boots. Caitlin loved pinks and vermilions. But she also liked to dress in black velvet with a chrysanthemum buried in her blonde hair, or a low-cut pink sweater with an orange scarf and a skirt of yet another color.

Cordelia and Harry Locke, who lived at the other end of South Leigh, often had beers with the Thomases at the Mason Arms, gave them use of their bath, and from time to time exchanged children and animals. Cordelia Locke writes of these days: "The drab, dreary six years of war were wiped out by a week of their company. Never were there such unexpected, flashing, kind, funny, maddening people! Only she could spin and dance round the room after a slogging day's work; only she would ask the young man to sing his Irish songs and really listen, as verse followed on tedious verse; and only she could draw people out who had shut the door on life long ago." Llewelyn Thomas was about the same age as the Lockes' daughter Nicola. On their first meeting they took to each other and, almost at once, went off together. Dylan noted their disappearance. "They're in bed already," he said, "wearing each other's vests." Dylan had a particular affection for Nicola; he once spent a whole evening cleaning a deep muddy cut in her foot. Years later she remembered his inexhaustible patience and sympathy as he sat with her leg propped on the table in front of him and a mug of beer at his side. "I was awfully silly and kept flinching and fidgeting," she said, "but he didn't bat an eyelid; just clucked and soothed me and went on until the cut was absolutely clean."[54]

In South Leigh, as usual, occurred the violent domestic scenes, the charges and countercharges that were a part

"Milk Wood" (Laugharne) and Sir John's Hill

of the Thomas family life. With his growing fame and his gift for
self-dramatization as a lost boy, Dylan had been attracting admirers
from the time he came up from the provinces. With her powerful
blonde beauty, Caitlin had been attracting admirers before she left
the provinces. In South Leigh incidents continued as before. Fiercely
devoted to Caitlin, Dylan was just as fiercely jealous of attentions
she evoked or provoked. Caitlin was devoted to Dylan, but she knew he
was not one to turn a cold shoulder to the advances of any woman.
Real or imagined intrusions by third parties were frequent, and
there often ensued knock-down, drag-out fights. The couple tended
to keep all their tenderness for their private relations; their anger
and outrage were exhibited in public. As Caitlin said of their domestic
battles, they

> were an essential part of our everyday life, and
> became fiercer and more deadly at each onslaught,
> so that you could have sworn no two people reviled
> each other more; and could never, under any
> fabulous change of circumstances, come together
> again: were almost worthwhile because, when the
> reconciliation did take place, according to how long
> we could stick it out, it was so doubly, trebly
> quadruply sweet, and we could never have ventured
> to conceive of such a thing happening again."[55]

Their term at South Leigh came to an end in March, 1949, when
Margaret Taylor purchased the beautifully situated Boat House
on the estuary of the River Taf in Laugharne, and offered it to
them. Both Caitlin and Dylan were happy at the notion of living
directly on the water—and Laugharne was the place of one of their
earliest meetings. Now it was to be their home for the final four
years of their lives together. A little house in town on the main
street, The Pelican, was to provide a home for D. J. and Florrie
Thomas. The whole family moved back to Wales, and on July 24 their
third child, Colm, arrived. All might have been well if there had been
someone to manage money matters. Dylan was not unwilling to do
miscellaneous writing to earn more. A few years earlier he had
answered a Horizon questionnaire on "The Cost of Letters" by saying,
among other things,

> I myself get about a quarter of the money I want
> by writing what I don't want to write and at the same
> time trying to, and often succeeding in, enjoying it.
> Shadily living by one's literary wits is as good a
> way of making too little money as any other, so long

as, all the time you are writing BBC and
film-scripts, reviews, etc., you aren't thinking,
sincerely, that this work is depriving the world of a
great poem or a great story.[56]

At one point he was so sadly harried by demands for back income tax
(of which he had no comprehension) that 90 per cent of every
pound he earned went to the Inland Revenue. He suffered torments of
anxiety because of his inability to manage money, often making
himself physically sick over the problem. Caitlin describes these times
in 1949: "The back debts went on pressing, only harder, getting
steadily more voracious; and the future was laden with threats and
wangling tortures: all the belittling intricacies of money worries. Poor
nervous Dylan, who had inherited, besides his father's hypochondria,
his acid pessimism for always anticipating the worst, suffered
sleepless nights more than me."[57] One brief and pleasant escape,
for Dylan at least, was a trip behind the Iron Curtain.

In Prague; Politics

Dylan had become friendly with the Cultural Attaché of the
Czechoslovakian Embassy in London, Aloys Skoumal, a Catholic
Socialist who had a passion for Jonathan Swift and liked to quote him
on any occasion. Through this acquaintance Dylan received an
invitation to attend a meeting to help establish the Communist
Writers' Union in Prague in March, 1949, which he accepted. There
Dylan developed an instant friendship with Vitezslav Nezval, the jovial
Czech poet and novelist. Nezval, fourteen years older than Dylan,
had as a young man lived for a time in Paris and in the Soviet Union,
after which he had returned to Czechoslovakia and became an
advocate of Breton and Apollinaire, Surrealism and Futurism. His
book, The Smaller Rose Garden (1927), was full of poetical fireworks:
fantastic rhymes, illogical chains of association, and grotesque
fancies. Having early developed a sympathy for communism, he wrote
Marxist propaganda, and eventually, in 1945, became head of the
Czech Ministry of Information. In many ways Nezval and Dylan
were alike: indifferent to the world of ideas and intellectual
abstraction, both loved boisterous schoolboy jokes and low life, and
both were excellent poets in a particularly modern idiom. In Prague,
according to an acquaintance, Dylan showed his usual disdain for
the facts of money: putting down a five-crown note (worth about a
dime) for his "double slivovice," he would say to the bartender "you
may keep the change."[58] Also in Prague, he became so disgusted with

his translator, whom he regarded as a dully literal-minded woman,
that he got up on the Charles Bridge, embraced one of the statues
and swore that he would jump into the river unless she were
banished. But Dylan fell in love with Prague, with its great castle
glooming above the city. It was, after all, the city of Kafka. The daily
gray pall that hung over everything reminded him of a Welsh
Sunday, but he was enthusiastic about the conference because it
seemed to him that men of good will were meeting congenially despite
the "cold war" machinations of the politicians. He became somewhat
disillusioned about the occasion when, in the course of events, his
friend Nezval fell into political disgrace with the directors of the
conference and was not permitted to give his speech at the final
session, as had been arranged.

    Dylan was not a member of the Communist Party,
despite the assertions of Augustus John and others. He had many
friends who were at that time members of the Party or close to it—
Jack Lindsay, Edgell Rickword, John Sommerfield, and Randall
Swingler. Having friends in the Party was a natural consequence of
having come of age in the early thirties when, for many young
intellectuals, communism was the most attractive theoretical solution
to world problems. In 1934, Geoffrey Grigson circulated a New Verse
questionnaire among some two dozen of the principal writers
asking, among other things, "Do you take your stand with any political
or politico-economic party or creed?" A majority of the writers
answered no, but many did take a definite stand. Gavin Ewart said,
"Yes, Communism." David Gascoyne said, "I have the strongest
possible sympathy with left-wing revolutionary movements." Hugh
MacDiarmid said, "I am a member of the Communist Party." Norman
Cameron said, "I believe that Communism is necessary and good,
but I'm not eager for it." Dylan said: "I take my stand with any
revolutionary body that asserts it to be the right of all men to share,
equally and impartially, every production of man from man and
from the sources of production at man's disposal, for only through
such an essentially revolutionary body can there be the possibility of
a communal art." More than once Dylan had said to Jack Lindsay,
"If all the party-members were like you and John Sommerfield,
I'd join up on the spot." But the fact is that he did not.

    At nineteen, when he had been writing to Pamela
Johnson, he told her that the hope of Revolution was then uppermost
in every thinking person's mind. He made a promise (not carried
out) to give her a reasoned outline of Revolution, the hard facts of
communism, in hopes that she would don her scarlet tie and

Playing Nap with Ebbie and Ivy Williams

"One front tooth broken after
playing a game called
Cats and Dogs in the Mermaid,
Mumbles"

carry the light to her fellow-writers in Hampstead.

Continuing his political and economic theorizing, he noted that human labor in industry was almost obsolete. He felt that the economic system was ethically bad, and went so far as to say (in 1933) that if the regular government could not fulfill its policies in the space of a year after the next General Election, then the Army and the police force would have to be subdued, and property be taken by force. He looked toward a classless society that would be neither an economic despotism nor a Christian utopia but a state of Functional Anarchy. This was the teen-ager's view. By 1935 he had encountered people representing a great many shades of political opinion, from the most conservative to the very left-wing, and had been rather disillusioned by his contact with the communists. He wrote to his old Socialist friend Bert Trick that he had met Morton, editor of the Daily Worker, and other leaders of the literary left wing including the editor of the communist monthly Out of Bounds, and other communist literary figures—and disliked all of them, not as persons but as revolutionaries. He felt that, because they were born in wealthy homes and educated at expensive schools, they had no real understanding of the class struggle—they were merely using politics as a subject for their literary activities. He announced firmly that he never wanted to be mixed up in the political ramifications of literary or pseudo-literary London. He said that honest writing does not mix with it. A writer has to be true to party or poetry. And, he concluded, the one social and economic creed that endures is poetry.

Despite this assertion of noninvolvement, Dylan's sympathy with the left-wing was continuous throughout his life. As early as 1934 he had written a letter to the editor of the Swansea and West Wales Guardian, attacking the fascist-minded inhabitants of Swansea. He gave his poetry free of charge to the leftist periodical Our Time, in which "Ceremony After a Fire Raid" was published in May, 1944. The Socialist point of view appeared again in his answer to one of the Horizon questions in 1946: Do you think the State or any other institution should do more for writers?

> The State should do no more for writers than it
> should do for any other person who lives in it.
> The State should give shelter, food, warmth, etc.
> whether the person works for the State or not. Choice
> of work and the money that comes from it, should
> then be free for that man; what work, what money, is
> his own bother.[59]

Still later he was to sign the Stockholm Peace Petition and the

Petition for Clemency for the Rosenbergs.

      The trip to Prague was really not so much political
as social. And it was but a moment of distraction from the domestic
and professional worries that awaited him back in Laugharne.

In America

Dylan had been dreaming of coming to America for more than five
years. Back in the days of New Quay, the American anthologist Oscar
Williams had been in correspondence with him about permission
to reprint certain poems, and Dylan had written that when the end of
the war came, which in 1945 seemed imminent, he wanted to come to
America, and he wondered how he might earn a living there: "I can
read aloud, through sonorous asthma, with pomp; I can lecture
on the trend of Y, or X at the crossroads, or Z: Whither? with an
assurance whose shiftiness can be seen only from the front row; I can
write script and radio films, of a sort; I can—and so on with the
list that could be, and is, supplied by every person fit for nothing but
his shameful ability to fit into the hack ends of commercial,
intellectual, or personal, advertisement."[60]

      John Malcolm Brinnin, the American poet, had also
learned of Dylan's wish to come to America. After trying unsuccessfully
for years to find some academic or literary institution, or some
wealthy person, who might sponsor a visit, he found himself
personally in a position to issue the invitation. This came about
through his having been appointed Director of the Poetry Center of
the Young Men's and Women's Hebrew Association of New York.

      When Brinnin offered Dylan two remunerative
appearances at the Poetry Center and his own services in securing
subsequent reading engagements, Dylan was eager to accept. With
his total inability to handle money and his tendency to become
confused about the time and place of his appointments, he needed
someone who could organize matters efficiently and who also had the
sensitivity to understand the human problems involved. Dylan wrote,
"I don't want to work my head off, but, on the other hand, I do
want to return to England with some dollars in my pocket. And, of
course, I want to get around the States a bit. I'll have to leave
this to you. I hand the baby over, with bewildered gratitude. . . .
I far prefer reading other chaps' work to my own: I find it clearer. An
hour of me aloud is hell, and produces large burning spots in
front of the mind. . . . Personally, I shall be glad to read anything—
and will certainly do my best to make it entertaining—except poems

John Malcolm Brinnin

in dialect, hymns to Stalin, anything over 500 lines. . . . Laughlin
[of New Directions] says there will be a party for me at the Gotham
Book Mart as soon as I get there: I shall polish up my glass belly."[61]

He arrived at Idlewild Airport on February 21, 1950,
and thus began the saga of the last three and a half years of his
life, which has been thoroughly and accurately documented in
Brinnin's Dylan Thomas in America. With Brinnin on his first day in
New York he quickly found two old friends, the poet Ruthven Todd and
the film-maker Len Lye, both of whom were living in Greenwich
Village. At an impromptu luncheon party the three rehearsed the
stories of prodigious drinking bouts in Soho that had laid everyone
under the table and of pub-crawls that never ended. When Len Lye's
wife Jane joined them, she took one look at the new arrival, whom
she had not seen in ten years, and wailed, "Oh Dylan—the last time
I saw you, you were an angel." And the change that had overtaken
Dylan can easily be seen in pictures from the two periods. The
photograph Dylan had forwarded for use on the Poetry Center
announcement showed a ravaged man. His thick hair was matted,
his widely separated teeth brown with tobacco stains, his flesh
paunchy; and there was a look of anxiety in his eyes. Several times on
the morning of his arrival he fell into fits of coughing that racked
his entire body. When asked what the trouble was, he replied, "I think
it's called cirrhosis of the liver." Throughout this first trip he was
to be in almost daily misery from spells of coughing that resulted in
vomiting and retching and, frequently, spitting of blood. This real
physical distress may have led him to the constant round of bars that
was to be his preoccupation in America and, as it turned out, his
condition was only made worse by this obsession. He had been at the
Beekman Towers Hotel only two nights when his drunken behavior
on returning late at night led the management to request that he find
quarters elsewhere.

His opening reading at the Poetry Center was
attended by more than a thousand people—the auditorium was
overflowing, with a maximum number of standees along the back.
With his magnificent voice and theatrical delivery, he read from Yeats,
Hardy, Auden, Lawrence, MacNeice, Alun Lewis, and Edith Sitwell.
He concluded the program with a selection from his own works,
moving from the tender and lyrical to the powerful and oratorical. He
gave a second reading at the Center that was an equal success,
then moved on to Yale, where he made his first appearance before a
college audience, and proceeded to Boston.

His first famous tour of American colleges was under

way. During the three months and one week that he was in America, he kept over thirty engagements, nearly all of them on college campuses. In order, they were the Y.M.H.A., Yale, Harvard, Mount Holyoke, Amherst, Bryn Mawr, Washington Institute of Contemporary Arts, Columbia, Cornell, Kenyon, Chicago, Notre Dame, Illinois, Iowa State, California (Berkeley), British Columbia, Washington (Seattle), California (Los Angeles), Pomona, Santa Barbara, Mills, San Francisco State, Cooper Union, Museum of Modern Art, Hobart, Florida, Wellesley, Brandeis, Michigan, Wayne State, Indiana, Vassar, Princeton, the Y.M.H.A., and Barnard. Of the various cities he visited, the three he liked best were San Francisco, Chicago, and Hollywood. These were the places where he felt least hemmed in by overzealous professors and the "ardents," as he called his fawning and idolatrous followers, places where he fell in with people sympathetic to his own personality and interests. In Chicago it was novelist Nelson Algren who introduced him to the ordinary bars of Chicago's South Side that otherwise he could hardly have known. In San Francisco it was a group of poets, Tram Combs, Kenneth Rexroth, Kenneth Patchen, Lawrence Ferlinghetti, and others, many of whom he met through Ruth Witt-Diamant's Poetry Center at the State College of San Francisco. Mrs. Witt-Diamant was to become his good friend, and later a close friend of Caitlin's. But the high point of the first visit to America occurred during his visit to the University of California at Los Angeles. The story is told by Brinnin:

> For part of his Hollywood visit he had been the guest of Christopher Isherwood. His report of the British novelist's life which, to Dylan, seemed to be all of a sun-baked ambience on the sands of southern California, was not without acid or without envy. When Isherwood had asked him what he wanted to do and whom he wanted to see, Dylan had told him that all his life long he had wanted to come to Hollywood for two reasons: to meet Charles Chaplin, and to have a date with an "ash-blonde" movie star. These wishes were both granted in one evening.
>
> The "ash-blonde" who became his partner at dinner with Isherwood and a small group of friends was Shelley Winters. While Dylan had not previously heard of her, she surprised him by remarks that showed she knew not only of him, but that she was acquainted with his work. Nevertheless, Dylan refused to address her by her given name—because,

he told her, that would be odd and upsetting.
Shortly after they had met, they had sat down for
drinks somewhere and, according to Dylan, talked
mostly of baseball, of which he knew nothing.
Eventually the conversation changed, becoming
centered in Dylan's appreciative enumeration of
Miss Winters' more obvious physical attractions,
which he had wanted to measure for himself. But he
was refused, he said, in language which was as
direct as a stevedore's and notably more colorful.

When they joined the dinner party at a Hollywood
restaurant, Frank Taylor, the well-known New York
editor who was then working with one of the movie
studios, phoned Charles Chaplin to tell him of
Dylan's great hope of meeting him. This resulted in
an invitation to come to Chaplin's home for the
evening. When the group arrived, they were greeted
with an impromptu commedia dell'arte performance
in which with a grace and skill at which Dylan
marveled, Chaplin travestied the manners of a
perfect host, a butler and a cloak-room maid.
Shaken by his contretemps with Miss Winters, who
herself had been made morose by the behavior of
this tipsy poet from Wales, Dylan was at first not
wholly in command of himself. But, before long,
exhilarated to hear Chaplin laughing at _his_ jokes, he
had bounced back. When he told his host that no one
back in Laugharne would believe him when
eventually he would tell of the visit, Chaplin
delighted him again by composing a cable and
sending it off directly to Caitlin.[62]

He met many of the American great and near-great on his travels:
he liked the salty talk of Carl Sandburg, he found Thornton
Wilder "completely endearing," he thought the future President
Eisenhower "nice enough," and he found himself at ease with
the cranky charms of E. E. Cummings. It was soon apparent in
America, as it had long been in England, that Dylan had a quality
which led anyone who had just met him to feel that he was an old
friend. But for all the hundreds of those who merely felt themselves
friends, there were many who actually became real friends—
Jean Garrigue, Jeanne Gordon Goldman, Pearl Kazin, Loren MacIver,
Lloyd Frankenburg, David Lougee, Stanley Moss, Theodore Roethke,

Dylan, Billy Williams, Caitlin, and Bill Read at
St. David's, Pembroke

Dylan's Shack on Cliff Walk

Caitlin with Aeron and Colm

and others. The first of Dylan's four trips to America ended on May 31, 1950. He had been ill continuously, yet in spite of this, had amply fulfilled two of his personae: the public professional poetry reader and the private romantic buffoon. Two other sides of his personality had not fared so well: the family man (he had not been able to conserve the money for his wife and children that had been one of the main reasons for the trip) and the poet (he had not found a way back into the writing of poetry that he had been seeking desperately for so long).

In Laugharne

The following summer, back in Laugharne, he worked on the poem "In the White Giant's Thigh" and saw the publication in England of the very posh edition of Twenty-Six Poems that had come out in America in May. This elegant little volume in black and green and white was printed on the hand press of the Officina Bodoni in Verona and consisted of 150 copies, all signed by the author, ten copies on vellum, the remainder on handmade paper, selling for $25 and $15 respectively: the entire issue was sold out on publication day.

That fall Dylan did some work for the BBC—in August he discussed the work of American poets, in September read three poems of his own, and in December engaged in a discussion of poetic license with George Barker, Roy Campbell, and W. R. Rodgers. In the spring he did a radio program on Persian oil. This curious choice of topic came about as a result of his having been commissioned by the company now known as the British Petroleum Company to prepare a propaganda movie. He was flown to Persia in January, 1951, and he wrote in a letter:

> The Anglo-Iranian Oil Company sent me out to write a film script to show how beautiful Persia is and how little as a mouse and gentle is the influence there of that Company: my job was to help pour water on troubled oil. I got out just before martial law —a friend of marshall plan's—and perhaps, disguised, will be sent back to write a script to show, now, suddenly, how beastly Persia is and how grandly irreplaceable is that thundering Company.[63]

The film was never made, for obvious reasons, and he wrote again later to Brinnin:

> No, Persia wasn't all depressing. Beautiful Ispahan and Shiraz. Wicked, pompous, oily British.

The Thomases at St. David's

The family

>Nervous, cunning, corrupt and delightful Persian
>bloody bastards. Opium no good. Persian vodka,
>made of beetroot, like stimulating sockjuice, very
>enjoyable. Beer full of glycerine and pips. Women
>veiled, or unveiled ugly, or beautiful and entirely
>inaccessible, or hungry. The lovely camels who sit on
>their necks and smile. I shan't go there again.[64]

Money was coming in from various sources: There were several
broadcasts as actor or reader; Marguerite Caetani, the editor
of the international literary magazine Botteghe Oscure, had
personally helped him; Bertram Rota, the book dealer, and others
were selling copies of poems in Dylan's handwriting to collectors for
him; royalties from Dent and New Directions were continuous. Yet,
despite these and numerous other sources of funds—his house was
provided by Margaret Taylor, and other friends frequently responded
to his pleading—there was a continuing financial crisis. Money simply
went out more rapidly than it came in. The sort of request for cash
that Vernon Watkins had begun receiving back in 1936 went to
others now with increasing desperation. In May of 1951 he wrote, "I'm
in such a state of debt and brokeness, I'm having to sell up my
house as soon as I can and move to London which I hate. The house—
what I own of it—will go towards debts—and then not all of them, by
a hell of a long way. I hope to keep my books. Oh, oh, oh! Misery me."
The eternal money problem only exacerbated his very real ill-health:
"I have gout, strained back, bronchitis, fits, and a sense of disaster,
otherwise very ill."[65]

Yet for all these feelings of despair—over money,
health, and not being able to write with the fluency that had been so
marvelous at the age of nineteen and that was never to return—
he was not unproductive. In the afternoons he would go to his
workshop, a little gardener's toolhouse perched precipitously on a cliff
a few hundreds yards from the Boat House. He called it his "shack"
or sometimes his "log cabin." About nine feet square, it had a
stove, a bookcase, and a work table in front of a large window looking
east out over the estuary of the Taf and the Towy Rivers to the sea.
The floor was normally littered with the discarded versions of poems.
The walls were covered with pictures clipped from magazines:
Edward Thomas, Frank Harris, a youthful Edith Sitwell, Marianne
Moore. There were reproductions of a Chinese painting, a
Cartier-Bresson photograph of Mexicans crowned with thorns, a
French Renaissance treatment of le beau tétin, an Italian primitive,
a photo of huge Indian street dolls, a Rouault, and many others. There

We are free to die like sky

Alone with the living,

FREE

It is hard to understand
That ~~of~~ the ... ker of the ~~sea~~ sea
And the air & the load
Is me;
~~It~~ But there is something understand:
I am not free.

The ~~cage goes~~ left went the 36 th
up to 6 floors ~~The last, I said, is my age.~~
And when the light ~~man~~ opened that door
I entered another cage.

Notes for "Poem on His Birthday"

Do Not Go Gentle Into That Good Night.

Do not go gentle into that good night,
Old age should burn and rave at close of day;
Rage, rage against the dying of the light.

_I_

Though wise men at their end know dark is right,
Because their words had forked no lightning they
Do not go gentle into that good night.

Good men, the last wave by, sighing how bright
Their frail deeds might have danced in a green bay,
Rage, rage against the dying of the light.

_(We)_
Wild men who caught and sang the sun in flight,
And learn, too late, they grieved it on its way,
Do not go gentle into that good night.

Grave
All men, near death, who see   with blinding sight
Blind   could blaze like fireflies and be gay
their eyes that could have naturedinto decay,
                           meteors

Rage, rage against the dying of the light.

Manuscript of "Do Not Go Gentle"

in the "shack" every afternoon he would try to settle down to his
new "Poem on His Birthday." Before he began the poem at all, he had
the plan all worked out: it was to be about a poet who realizes he
has arrived at "half his bible span." He means both to celebrate and
spurn his birthday in a house high among trees, overlooking the sea.
Birds and fishes move under and around him on their dying ways,
and he, a craftsman in words, toils "towards his own wounds which
are waiting in ambush for him." The poet "sings in the direction
of his pain." Birds fly after the hawks that will kill them. Fishes swim
toward the otters that will eat them. He sees herons walking in
their shrouds, which is the water they fish in; and he, who is
progressing, afraid, to his own fiery end in the cloud of an atomic
explosion knows that, out at sea, animals who attack and eat other
sea animals are tasting the flesh of their own death. Now exactly half
of his three score and ten years has gone. He looks back at his times
—his loves, his hates, all he has seen—and sees the logical
progress of death in everything he has been and done. His death lurks
for him, and for all, in the next lunatic war. And, still singing, still
praising the radiant earth, still loving, though remotely, the animal
creation also gladly pursuing their inevitable and grievous ends, he
goes toward his. Why should he praise God and the beauty of the
world, as he moves to horrible death? He does not like the deep zero
dark, and the nearer he gets to it, the louder he sings, the higher
the salmon leaps, the shriller the birds carol.

In addition to the "Poem on His Birthday," Dylan
was also working on two other poems, which were to be published in
the November Botteghe Oscure. One was "Lament," the lament of
a playboy who married a virtuous wife—a poem which the BBC
on one occasion was to ban from the air for "bawdiness." The
other was "Do Not Go Gentle into That Good Night," written
for his father. As early as 1934 D. J. Thomas had had to submit to
needle-injection treatment for cancer of the throat, his heart had
gradually weakened, and the sternness of his early life had
disappeared. No longer the awe-inspiring schoolmaster, he had
become a sweet and longsuffering old man. His condition continued
to worsen, and on December 16, 1952, he died.

Just before his own death, Dylan was working on a
second poem for his father which was ultimately completed by
Vernon Watkins. The son's admiration for the man appears in the
notes he made for that longer poem:

Although he was too proud to die, he did die,
blind, in the most agonizing way, but he did not
flinch from death and was brave in his pride.

In his innocence, and thinking he was God-hating,
he never knew that what he was was: an old kind
man in his burning pride.

His mother said that as a baby he never cried;
nor did he as an old man; he just cried to his
secret wound, and his blindness, never aloud.[66]

The elder Thomas had had many reasons both to curse and bless
his son. He had hoped for a student who would go on to a university
and become an educated gentleman. But, on other other hand, he
was himself a poet manqué, and it was a kind of glory to live to see
his son an internationally celebrated poet who said

Do Not Go Gentle Into That Good Night

Do not go gentle into that good night,
Old age should burn and rave at close of day;
Rage, rage against the dying of the light.

Though wise men at their end know dark is right,
Because their words had forked no lightning they
Do not go gentle into that good night.

Good men, the last wave by, crying how bright
Their frail deeds might have danced in a green bay,
Rage, rage against the dying of the light.

Wild men who caught and sang the sun in flight,
And learn, too late, they grieved it on its way,
Do not go gentle into that good night.

Grave men, near death, who see with blinding sight
Blind eyes could blaze like meteors and be gay,
Rage, rage against the dying of the light.

And you, my father, there on the sad height,
Curse, bless, me now with your fierce tears, I pray.
Do not go gentle into that good night.
Rage, rage against the dying of the light.

Dylan

In America II

In October Dylan had sent the first half of Llareggub to Marguerite Caetani, asking for £100 to pay for the whole work. He said that the Boat House had to be sold (which was not true), and that they were being forced to leave for London to live in a borrowed flat. The new flat was in London's Camden Town, 54 Delancey Street, "a house of horror on bus and night-lorry route and opposite railway bridge and shunting station. No herons here."[67]

  Dylan and Caitlin were glad enough to leave this dreariness in midwinter to board the Queen Mary and head for America for the second visit, which was to last for three months and three weeks, January 20 to May 16, 1952. John Brinnin met them in New York and took them to the country home of his friend the photographer Mrs. Rosalie Thorne McKenna in Millbrook, New York. Caitlin has described her: "There was his friend Rollie; the least American in the vacuum-cleaner sucking-up sense, of anybody we met; she was most refreshing after the douches of gush that were later released over Dylan's unbowed head. I wanted nothing better than to spend the rest of my life in her cool, unpossessive company."[68] Caitlin, as usual, was very dashing, dressed in a black fur hat, carrying a big fur muff, and wearing fur-tipped boots. Dylan was feeling well for the moment, and at Millbrook Rollie took a whole series of pictures that became part of her famous collection of poets' portraits. Then there were quiet drives about the countryside, a visit to Vassar where Caitlin had her first sight of blue-jeaned college girls who, she said, looked like "intellectual witches." Over cocktails at Rollie's house, Caitlin made a whole series of caricatures of the group; the one of Dylan, reproduced here, was drawn on a flattened box of Between the Acts, the little cigars he had discovered in America and liked so well.

  Back in New York, they settled into a one-room kitchenette apartment at the Hotel Chelsea that the painter Loren MacIver had helped Caitlin pick out. The second American reading tour got under way, opening at the Poetry Center of the YMHA.

  There followed another trip across the country: Columbia, YMHA, Museum of Modern Art, Washington I.C.A., New School for Social Research, N.Y.U., Vermont, Museum of Modern Art, N.Y.U., Cherry Lane Theatre, Bennett Jr. College, McGill, N. Y. Socialist Party, Washington I.C.A., Johns Hopkins, Princeton, M.I.T., DeCordova Museum, Poets' Theatre (Cambridge), Boston University,

New School for Social Research, Skidmore, Circle-in-the-Square, Penn State, San Francisco State, British Columbia, Washington (Seattle), California (Berkeley), San Francisco Museum of Art, Utah, Missouri, Poetry Magazine, Northwestern, Marquette, N.Y. Masters Institute, Washington I.C.A., Connecticut, Bard, Sarah Lawrence, Dartmouth, Duncan Phillips Gallery, and back to the Poetry Center for a final triumphant reading mid-May. This second expedition had started well. Caitlin had found good friends in sculptor David Slivka and his wife Rose and in Mrs. Frances Brinnin, and Dylan had found an increasing circle of admirers—as well as the White Horse Tavern, perhaps the closest thing to a British pub in America. But Dylan's financial irresponsibility was compounded by Caitlin's spendthrift ways, and the large sums of money earned weekly vanished daily. Dylan would spend $75 in a day and not be able to account for any of it. Caitlin would spend $40 to have a bundle of laundry mailed to her. And, although thousands of dollars were earned, all but a few hundred had disappeared before they were ready to sail home in May.

It was on this trip, on February 22, 1952, that Dylan made his first extensive commercial recording of his poems. Two recent college graduates, the present Mrs. Barbara Holdridge and Mrs. Marianne Mantell, had decided that winter to form a company to be called Caedmon Records to publish spoken recordings of literary works, and Dylan's readings were to make up their first record. This first session at midnight in Steinway Hall was followed by a second in May, 1953. From these two sessions came the material for the first two long-playing records of Dylan's readings. Several years earlier he had recorded "The War Song of Dinas Vawr" and "The Three Wise Men of Gotham" (both by one of his favorite authors Thomas Love Peacock) for the London Library of Recorded English, and in the summer of 1949 he recorded his own "Poem in October" and "In My Craft and Sullen Art" for Lloyd Frankenberg's Columbia record Pleasure Dome. Since the first two Caedmon records, nine more have been made from the tape recordings of the Y.M.H.A., the Massachusetts Institute of Technology, and the Boston radio station WGBH.

In February, too, his six poems In Country Sleep were published by New Directions, 5000 copies of the regular —and beautiful—edition, 100 copies on special paper signed by the author. But this created only a small splash compared with the Collected Poems which appeared in November in England, and in America the following March. This was also brought out in two versions—the regular edition was supplemented by sixty-five copies

Chelsea Hotel, New York

Caitlin's caricature of Dylan

Dylan with small cigar

bound in blue morocco, numbered, and signed by the author.
The volume was an immediate success. Philip Toynbee said, "It need
no longer be eccentric to claim that Thomas is the greatest living
poet in the English language." Though there were critics, particularly
in England, who disagreed, the book-buying public tended to support
Toynbee's view. But, curiously, the book's success did not seem to
mean a great deal to the author. The head of J. M. Dent, his English
publisher, Mr. E. F. Bozman, has commented:

> Courteous in manner, soft-spoken and persuasive
> in conversation, apparently business-like, without
> any sign of self-importance and grateful for and
> mildly surprised at anything that was done for him
> commercially, he could nevertheless be counted on
> to miss every opportunity that came his way for
> making a practical success of his authorship and to
> set at naught every effort that was made to persuade
> him to help himself. It was as if the everyday
> successes of the writer only touched the surface of
> him—as if there was something else in his mind
> that mattered far more than the ordinary human
> satisfactions. He would flip through a bundle of
> "rave" reviews, treating them like the products of a
> children's competition—let the critics have their
> little games, his manner indicated, it's nothing to do
> with me. Even his own poetry, of which he was very
> fond indeed, he had no desire to understand. In fact
> he used to say that he couldn't be expected to do
> so. Hadn't he written it? Surely that was enough
> to ask of anyone.
>
> Undoubtedly the publishing event that meant
> most to him was the issue of his Collected Poems.
> But in putting them together, and revising them, he
> lost all interest periodically, even going so far as to
> lose the actual material on several occasions, and
> when the book proved to be an outstanding success,
> he was neither elated nor surprised.
>
> . . . his letters to his publishers were regular and
> practical, unless some work was proposed that
> appeared to be particularly in his commercial
> interest, in which case he would not answer at all.
> Appointments he did not as a rule keep—and having
> failed in this respect he would go to immense

personal troubles to apologize and put the matter right, exercising an anxious and disarming approach which preserved him the right to repeat the performance.[69]

In the fall of 1952 and early 1953, Dylan was occupied with broadcasting for the BBC (which included writing an introduction for and selecting an anthology of poems from Edgar Lee Masters), doing some reviewing, and preparing the scenario of The Doctor and the Devils for publication. Throughout the winter he dealt with the recurring problem of whether or not he ought to make a third trip to America. The first two trips had been tremendously rewarding by way of a personal recognition that had never been granted in England on such a wide scale. They had proved that he could get large sums of money in a very short time. The fact that money did not accumulate was merely a manifestation of a lifelong dilemma. A second source of trouble was the matter of Dylan's philandering. While he was deeply devoted to his wife and while his escapades were temporary indeed, Caitlin was fiercely jealous. She said that he wanted to go to the States for "flattery, idleness and infidelity." He insisted the right words were "appreciation, dramatic work, and friends."

The financial problem continued its grinding way: now that his father's schoolteacher pension was no more, Dylan was for the first time faced with financial responsibility for his mother, and both Llewelyn (at Magdalen College School, Oxford) and Aeron (at Arts Educational School, Tring Park, Herts.) were in schools that required tuition payments. The publishers who had advanced him money for A Bard's Eye View of the U.S.A., which he had never written, had threatened to set the law on him (at least so Dylan said) if he did not produce the book by a certain date.

The tenor of these days, as the various horrors of Dylan's life mounted, is sadly clear from this letter to Marguerite Caetani, to whom he apologized for not having sent the rest of Llareggub, and for not even having written to her.

[Nov. 6, 1952] . . . I grew more and more ashamed of my silence and more angry with my procrastination until, at last, I couldn't write at all. I buried my head in the sands of America; flew over America like a damp, ranting bird; boomed and fiddled while home was burning; carried with me all the time, my unfinished letters, my dying explanations and self-accusations, my lonely half of

a looney maybe-play, in a heavy, hurtful bunch.
These ostrich griefs were always with me, and
whispered loudest in the late night when, indeed, I
was all sand. . . . These pages, I think, are wilting
in the grey nearly permanent drizzle that sighs down
on to this town and through the birdscratched
matchboard roof into my worksplashed hut. It isn't
rain, it must be remorse. The whole fishy bay is
soaked in guilt like the bad bits of poems-not-to-be
oozing to the marrow on the matchsticked floor, and
the half-letters curling and whining in the warped
drawers. I'm writing this guilty noise in a cold pool,
on a November afternoon, in mists of depression.
. . . When I try to explain my fear, the confused
symbols grow leaden and a wooly rust creeps over
the words. . . . One instinct of fear is to try to make
oneself as little, as unnoticeable, as possible, to
cower, as one thinks, unseen and anonymous until
the hunt is past. My fearful instinct is to bloat myself
like a frog, to magnify my unimportance, to ring a
bell for a name, so that, as I bluster and loom twice
my size, the hunt, seeing me monstrous, bays by
after different and humble prey. But that is not
what I mean; the symbols have wet-brain, the words
have swallowed their tongues.

[After you, Mme. Caetani, helped me to pay off
my Laugharne debts, I went off to London] which, to
me, is nowhere, and lived by odd reviews—and
they were odd, too—odder broadcasts, pretending
to women's clubs. . . . Then I went to the States
with my luggage of dismays and was loudly lost for
months, peddling and bawling to adolescents the
romantic agonies of the dead. I made money, and
it went, and I returned with none . . . and once
more . . . reviewed, begged, lectured, broadcast. . . .

It is so difficult for me to live and keep my family
alive. There are many petty jobs which would make
me just not enough money for tradesmen and rent,
for clothes and school, for parents, shoes, and
cigarettes, but these petty jobs by their nature
and by the time they claim, stop me writing as I
could wish to write. But how, without these jobs,

Llewelyn Edouard Thomas

Aeron Thomas

am I to live, to write, at all? These problems keep me
treadmilling small nightmares all the waking nights.
. . . I cannot go on thinking all the time of butchers
and bakers and grocers and cobblers and rates and
rents until I bleed. After I have finished what I am
now working on, I may have to give up writing
altogether. My need—as I imagine it—to write,
may be all conceit. The bellows that fan the little
flicker is nothing but wind, after all. And writing is
certainly not one of the ancient secrets of the
head-shrinking tribes. Ach, my endless bleating of
private woes because I am not "allowed" to write,
as though the trees would grow inward, like
toenails, if I renounced this passion for
self-glorification. "Peace, let me write. Gag the
tradesmen, I must write. Alms, for the love of
writing." Perhaps I should be better off pulling
teeth.[70]

In December he asked Stephen Spender if he would raise another
fund like the one that was so successful in 1940, but most of
the people Spender wrote replied that Dylan's income was now
larger than their own. All of the problems eventually found their
temporary solutions. Caitlin was totally opposed to the third trip;
but Dylan had discovered in America a source of satisfaction that he
could not find in England and was determined to make it, one way or
another. One possibility, considered and rejected, was to bring
Caitlin and Colm to America, go on a short reading tour, and then to
find a house in America and some kind of work other than
"cross-continental reading and raving." The solution arrived at, after
considerable misery on everyone's part, was that he was to go for a
much shorter trip—not three months as before, but just six weeks. In
that time he was to pile up enough cash to permit him, Caitlin, and
Colm to go to Portugal for the winter where it would be cheap and
sunny.

In America III

Crossing on the SS United States, Dylan arrived in New York on
April 21, 1953, and went at once to his favorite Chelsea Hotel and his
favorite bar, the White Horse Tavern on Hudson Street. His chief
concern was to bring into actable condition the play he had long been
working on. His readings took him in and out of Boston where,

staying with John Brinnin at 100 Memorial Drive, he found peace to work from time to time on the play, looking out of the picture window over the Charles River Basin toward the gold dome of the State House. He made trips to Bennington, Syracuse, and Williams colleges, then came back to Boston for his one-man performance of Under Milk Wood. This world première of the play was sponsored by the Poet's Theatre of Cambridge and was performed at the Fogg Museum on May 3, 1953.

The origin of Milk Wood lay in an idea Dylan had come upon in those miraculous few years in Swansea, 1933 and 1934, when, seemingly, the seeds of his entire career germinated and took deep root—to evolve gradually into a masterpiece during the succeeding twenty years of his life. When he was on the sands of Caswell Bay talking to Bert and Nell Trick, he used to tell of the sketch he had in mind, centered on a row of terrace houses in a Welsh seaside town—the different residents were to come out of their doors revealing their behavior and thoughts, and the village would be named Llareggub.

The next stage in its history was in 1945, when the BBC commissioned Dylan to do a radio piece. He was living in New Quay, Cardiganshire, at the time, and the idea of his earlier description of a small Welsh town recurred. Thus the original motif of Swansea, modified by his residence in Laugharne beginning in 1938, was further modified by his residence in New Quay in 1945. When the prose version was completed it was called "Quite Early One Morning": "Quite early one morning in the winter in Wales, by the sea that was lying down still and green as grass after a night of tar-black howling and rolling, I went out of the house, where I had come to stay for a cold unseasonable holiday, to see if it was raining still, if the outhouse had been blown away, potatoes, shears, rat-killer, shrimpnets, and tins of rusty nails aloft on the wind, and if all the cliffs were left." This early version contains the whole plan of the play in embryo. There is the same time range, though the hours are limited to the morning and the season is winter rather than spring. The sleeping town dreams, and the sleepers get up and go about their business. Even some of the later lines are here, as when the lady gives instructions to her two husbands: "I am Mrs. Ogmore-Pritchard and I want another snooze. Dust the china, feed the canary, sweep the drawing-room floor. And before you let the sun in, mind he wipes his shoes."

This prose radio piece was such a success that Dylan decided to give it a more extended treatment. He wavered between

Citizens of Laugharne

At the bar of the White Horse Tavern

Elizabeth Reitell

Citizens of Laugharne

Cast of Under Milk Wood

doing it as a radio play and a stage play, and for a while planned to work a plot into it. Daniel Jones, who was later to compose the music, says that there was to be a conflict between Llareggub and the surrounding world—"between the eccentrics, strong in their individuality and freedom, and the sane ones who sacrifice everything to some notion of conformity. The whole population of Llareggub cannot very well be accommodated inside the walls of a lunatic asylum; so the sane world decrees that the town itself shall be declared an 'insane area,' with all traffic and goods diverted from it. Captain Cat, spokesman of the indignant citizens, insists that the sanity of Llareggub should be put on trial in the town hall with every legal formality; he will be Counsel for the Defense and the citizens themselves will be witnesses. The trial takes place, but comes to a surprising end. The final speech of the Prosecution consists of a full and minute description of the ideally sane town; as soon as they hear this, the people of Llareggub withdraw their defense and beg to be cordoned off from the sane world as soon as possible."[71]

By 1949, in the Boat House, Dylan was working seriously on The Town That Was Mad, its second title. But the plot framework seemed unnecessary, and he returned to the original lyrical pattern of the radio talk in order to make a radio, not a stage, play, and to use only the passage of a full day from dawn to dark to set the pattern of events. He wrote down his intention in 1951, saying that he wanted to make "a piece, a play, an impression for voices, an entertainment out of the darkness, of the town I live in, and to write it simply and warmly and comically with lots of movement and varieties of moods, so that, at many levels, through sight and speech, description and dialogue, evocation and parody, you come to know the town as an inhabitant of it."

The one-man performance of the play in Cambridge was to be followed in less than ten days by a full-cast performance with Dylan in the role of narrator in New York. John Brinnin had asked his assistant there, Elizabeth Reitell, to take charge as production manager for the rehearsal of the Poetry Center cast that was to work with Dylan. "Liz," as everyone called her, had recruited the actors and had begun rehearsals even before Dylan's arrival in America, and she worked closely with him after his arrival in preparing the show for its performance. Dylan, the perfectionist as ever in his craft, was still, even on the final day, working on the script at Rollie McKenna's New York apartment, not far from the YMHA. As John Brinnin describes it,

With two typists in attendance, they worked from five until seven. When new pieces of manuscript were finished, Dylan handed them to Liz, who looked them over, made the illegible parts legible, then handed them on to the typists. But in the middle of this frantic piecing and pruning, Dylan suddenly gave up. He was ill and weary, he said, he simply could not go on. Since the final third of the play was still unorganized and but partially written, Liz felt that the evening's performance would have to be called off, that she or I would have to go before the audience and make an announcement to that effect. When she expressed this to Dylan, he said it was unthinkable, absolutely unthinkable. He buckled down then, and in sober determination finished up one scene after another. In spite of every last-gasp effort he had finally to give up the thought of completing the work in time for its première. But in those last minutes he devised a tentative conclusion that would serve. Twenty minutes before curtain time, fragments of Under Milk Wood were still being handed to the actors as they applied make-up, read their telegrams and tested their new accents on one another. Some lines of dialogue did not actually come into the hands of the readers until they were already taking their places on stage.[72]

That performance on May 14, 1953, was a resounding success and, as a result of the Poetry Center's practice of taping all its poetry programs, is now, happily, available on phonograph records.

The public readings of poetry on this third trip included performances at Boston University, Bennington College, Syracuse University, Williams College, Cambridge Poets' Theatre, Washington I.C.A., Randolph-Macon Woman's College, Philadelphia Art Alliance, M.I.T., Duke University, University of Connecticut, Amherst College, and Y.M.H.A. Poetry Center. After the Amherst reading on May 20, Dylan returned to Boston to John Brinnin's apartment where he was, among other things, thinking about a new play. To be called Two Streets, the play would be set in a small industrial town in South Wales and would tell of the lives of two families who live unknown to each other in neighboring streets. The play would begin, not with words, but with screams—the screams of women in labor and of newborn babies: a boy to one of the families, a

Reading poetry

girl to the other. The boy and girl would live their separate but unconsciously interwoven lives at separate ends of the stage. They would live uneventfully, waiting for some fulfillment of their great capacity for life; and while, in the routine of their days and years, they pass close to one another hundreds of times, they never meet. Then at the very end, when it is all too late, they meet in a dance hall— the center of the stage. It was to be the love story of two people who were never to be lovers.

But the most exciting prospect in the future was an opera which was conceived in Boston. While Dylan was at the Brinnin apartment one day, he received a phone call from a representative of Igor Stravinsky, who had just finished conducting students of Boston University in a production of The Rake's Progress. Dean Robert A. Choate, head of the University's School of Fine and Applied Arts, had joined with the head of his Opera Department, Sarah Caldwell, to explore the possibilities of commissioning a new opera on behalf of the University. Stravinsky, who had been delighted with the quality of the music students with whom he had been working, agreed to the idea at once, and, when asked who he would like to have prepare the libretto, said, "There is only one person to do it—the best living writer—Dylan Thomas." Before the time set for his meeting with Stravinsky, Dylan had a plan for the libretto worked out. As he later explained it to Brinnin, it was to be a

> recreation of the world—an opera about the only man and woman alive on earth. These creatures might be visitors from outer space who, by some cosmic mischance, find themselves on an earth recently devastated and silenced by global warfare; or they might be earthlings who somehow have survived an atomic miscalculation. In either case, they would re-experience the whole awakening life of aboriginal man. They would make a new cosmogony. Confronted with a tree pushing its way upward out of radio-active dust, they would have to name it, and learn its uses, and then proceed to find names and a definition for everything on earth. The landscape would be fantastic—everything shaped and colored by the dreams of primitive man —and even the rocks and trees would sing.[73]

Dylan joined Miss Caldwell to meet the composer at the Boston Sheraton Plaza Hotel. Stravinsky was ill and confined to his bed on the appointed day, and Dylan was in a state of deep awe at the prospect of meeting Stravinsky. Their first exchanges were on a very formal level, until the older man said, "The reason I always stay at the Sheraton in Boston is that they have wonderful wine cellars. Would you care to have a drink?" The ice was broken, the discussion got under way, and each discovered that he liked the other enormously. Dylan wanted the music to have the power of "Le Sacre du Printemps", but Stravinsky was, at that time, experimenting with serial methods of composing, and would have used that style. Dylan would think about the project over the summer and plan to return in the fall to work directly with the composer at his Hollywood, California, home.

Everything about the opera was exploratory. The fees suggested as possible were $4000 for Dylan and $20,000 for Stravinsky. Dean Choate was going to try to raise the money through the B.U. Friends of Music, the patrons of the Boston University Music Department. And that was the way things were left. Stravinsky went on to build an extension on his house so that there would be a room for Dylan to live and work in. By the fall the University, hopefully, would have acquired the necessary funds and drawn up the formal contract. But that rich collaboration was never to be.

The End

After a final performance of Under Milk Wood at the YMHA on May 28, Dylan returned to the Boat House in Laugharne. During the summer he continued revising the play for publication and broadcasting, worked further on his novel Adventures in the Skin Trade (which had been under way since 1941), and toyed with further ideas for the opera. That September, Rollie McKenna and John Brinnin, who were vacationing in England, went to Laugharne to visit the Thomases and there Rollie added to the collection of photographs begun in Millbrook the year before. Dylan was now having blackouts at frequent intervals. On more than one occasion he had been warned by his doctor that he must go on a regime of complete abstinence from alcohol if he was to survive. In his earlier days in London he had been hospitalized on two or three occasions, and for brief periods after these sessions he did manage to stay away from drink, but never for long. Now the alcohol was beginning to tell, as capillaries of the brain collapsed, resulting in brief periods of unconsciousness. Again there were anguished discussions between Dylan and Caitlin as to whether or not it was advisable to go to America for this, the fourth time. Finally, it was decided that he

Directing <u>Under Milk Wood</u>

''Guilt and grief and illness''

"I've lived with it a long time and know it horridly
well and can't explain it"

would go ahead: he would give just a few highly paid readings to provide funds (in November he would sign a contract with an American agent that would guarantee him $1000 per week), and Caitlin and Colm would join him in California later.

So it was that on October 19, 1953, he flew to New York ready to direct rehearsals of the expanded Under Milk Wood. Although he was not well, he participated in the third and fourth performances of the play at the Y.M.H.A. and both were sensations. On Oct. 28 he gave a poetry reading at the City College of New York, and that evening participated in a Cinema 16 symposium on film art. One evening shortly after that as Liz Reitell and he were walking in Greenwich Village, Dylan spotted a huge billboard announcing a movie: Houdini. He called Liz' attention to it and said that the magician had always fascinated him because of his fabulous escapes from the many ingenious traps that he had allowed to be devised for him. The worst horror in life, Dylan said, the horror beyond horrors, was the sense of being hopelessly trapped. It was a subject he was going to write about; in fact, he said, he was already well along into a prose-piece about an "escape artist."

But there was to be no escape from his illness. He later had to leave a rehearsal, retching violently and finally falling to the floor. "I can't do anything any more," he said. "I'm too tired to do anything. I can't eat, I can't drink—I'm even too tired to sleep." He lay down on the couch. "I have seen the gates of hell tonight," he said. "Oh, but I do want to go on—for another ten years anyway. But not as a bloody invalid—not as a bloody invalid." He groaned and turned his face to the wall. "I'm too sick too much of the time."

Later on that evening, Liz came by the Chelsea Hotel with Herb Hannum, a frequent companion of Dylan's whom Liz would later marry. Dylan said to them, "I've come to the melancholy conclusion that my health is totally gone. I can't drink at all. I always could, before . . . but now most of the time I can't even swallow beer without being sick. I tell myself that if I'd only lay off whiskey and stick to beer I'd be all right . . . but I never do. I guess I just forgot to sleep and eat for too long. I'll have to give up something."

The intensity of his illness increased day after day through the end of October and the beginning of November. On November 3 Ruthven Todd and Herb Hannum dropped by the Chelsea Hotel for a morning visit. When they had left, Dylan and Liz Reitell spoke with the hopeful lecture agent about the contract stipulating

Caitlin

Caitlin, the widow

St. Martin's Churchyard, Laugharne

Welsh farmland

very large fees. Afterward Dylan seemed exhausted, self-preoccupied, and morbidly depressed. Nevertheless, that afternoon he and Liz attended a cocktail party at the home of Santha Rama Rau and her husband; but afterward he felt exhausted and could not join a theatre party that was to have included them. Instead they returned to the Chelsea where, in obvious agony of body and mind, he said to Liz, "I want to go to the Garden of Eden . . . to die . . . to be forever unconscious. . . . You know, I adore my little boy . . . I can't bear the thought that I'm not going to see him again. . . . He doesn't deserve this. . . . He doesn't deserve my wanting to die. I truly want to die." Speaking of Caitlin then, he said, "You have no idea how beautiful she is. There is an illumination about her . . . she shines." After some fitful sleep during which he murmured phrases of disconnected talk, he rose up and with a fierce look said, "I've got to have a drink." He went out alone, and an hour and a half later returned to announce, "I've had eighteen straight whiskies. I think that's the record."[74]

In the morning he awoke feeling, he said, as if he were suffocating. His illness became worse through the day; his friends called the physician he had consulted earlier, Dr. Milton Feltenstein. Medications gave him very little relief; the nausea and vomiting continued. In the late evening of Nov. 4 delirium had begun to set in. A call to Dr. Feltenstein brought an ambulance that took Dylan, now in a coma that was to last five days, to St. Vincent's Hospital.

In Laugharne that same evening, Caitlin was attending a meeting in the school hall at which a documentary program about the village was being broadcast. Dylan had provided a recorded tribute to the "timeless, beautiful" town where, he said, he had lived "for fifteen years, or centuries." As Aneirin Davies, who had arranged the event, was concluding the broadcast with a tribute to the poet, Caitlin was informed that her husband was lying unconscious in the hospital. She made arrangements to fly at once to New York, but by the time she arrived Dylan, still in a coma, had weakened to a point of death. On November 9 he died.

About four hundred people attended the memorial service in St. Luke's Episcopal Chapel of Trinity Parish in New York. Caitlin accompanied her husband's body back to Laugharne on the SS <u>United States</u>. The funeral, on November 24, began at his mother's home. Since the door was too narrow, six Laugharne friends bore the casket out through the front window to the waiting hearse. The cortege began with a car bearing Caitlin and Dylan's

"Time has ticked a heaven round the stars"

longtime Swansea friend Daniel Jones. His mother, bereaved of
husband, her daughter Nancy (in India), and now her son in less than
a year, was ill herself and did not go, but watched from the doorway.
The mourners walked from the house up the village road to
St. Martin's churchyard. Passing through a stone-roofed gateway,
they climbed a steep path a hundred yards up the hill to the medieval
parish church of St. Martin. The church was filled with Dylan's friends
and relatives, among them Mrs. Macnamara, Nicolette Macnamara
Devas, Louis MacNeice, Vernon Watkins, Alfred Janes, Margaret
Taylor, Ivy and Ebbie Williams, Aneirin Davies, Keidrych Rhys, John
Prichard, Thomas Fisher, Robert Pocock and John Davenport. The
service was simple: After a hymn, "Blessed Are the Pure in Heart,"
the Rev. J. R. Williams, rector of Pendine, read a psalm. The elderly
vicar of Laugharne, S. B. Williams, read St. Paul's remarks on death,
I Corinthians 15, and the service closed with a hymn, "Forever with
the Lord," and a prayer. Then the casket was taken from the altar
with its lighted candles, through the vine-deep churchyard, across
an ancient stone bridge, farther up the steep hillside, and placed
in the grave. Across the valley cattle and lambs grazed calmly. Nearby
the cocks suddenly began to crow vigorously, as if to announce a
beginning, to which Dylan was going, "for as long as forever is."

Fern Hill

Now as I was young and easy under the apple boughs
About the lilting house and happy as the grass was green,
    The night above the dingle starry,
      Time let me hail and climb
    Golden in the heydays of his eyes,
And honoured among wagons I was prince of the apple towns
And once below a time I lordly had the trees and leaves
      Trail with daisies and barley
    Down the rivers of the windfall light.

And as I was green and carefree, famous among the barns
About the happy yard and singing as the farm was home,
    In the sun that is young once only,
      Time let me play and be
    Golden in the mercy of his means,
And green and golden I was huntsman and herdsman, the calves
Sang to my horn, the foxes on the hills barked clear and cold,
      And the sabbath rang slowly
    In the pebbles of the holy streams.

All the sun long it was running, it was lovely, the hay
Fields high as the house, the tunes from the chimneys, it was air
    And playing, lovely and watery
        And fire green as grass.
    And nightly under the simple stars
As I rode to sleep the owls were bearing the farm away,
All the moon long I heard, blessed among stables, the night-jars
    Flying with the ricks, and the horses
        Flashing into the dark.

And then to awake, and the farm, like a wanderer white
With the dew, come back, the cock on his shoulder: it was all
    Shining, it was Adam and maiden,
        The sky gathered again
    And the sun grew round that very day.
So it must have been after the birth of the simple light
In the first, spinning place, the spellbound horses walking warm
    Out of the whinnying green stable
        On to the fields of praise.

And honoured among foxes and pheasants by the gay house
Under the new made clouds and happy as the heart was long,
    In the sun born over and over,
        I ran my heedless ways,
    My wishes raced through the house high hay
And nothing I cared, at my sky blue trades, that time allows
In all his tuneful turning so few and such morning songs
    Before the children green and golden
        Follow him out of grace,

Nothing I cared, in the lamb white days, that time would take me
Up to the swallow thronged loft by the shadow of my hand,
    In the moon that is always rising,
        Nor that riding to sleep
    I should hear him fly with the high fields
And wake to the farm forever fled from the childless land.
Oh as I was young and easy in the mercy of his means,
        Time held me green and dying
        Though I sang in my chains like the sea.

Dylan

Welsh countryside

Concerning The Names

The pronunciation of Welsh names is notoriously difficult for the outsider; the following notes, however, may be of help in pronouncing the most frequent names in the text. Dylan rhymes, as he confirmed, with "chillun," despite the fact that the Welsh generally pronounce the name "dullen." The first syllable of Caitlin rhymes with "cat," not "Kate." Aeron rhymes with "Byron." Colm sounds like "column." Rhossilli is pronounced "ross-silly" with the accent on the second syllable. Gower rhymes with "bower." Cwmdonkin is "koom-don'kin." Llangain is accented on the second syllable, which rhymes with "mine"; the roughness of the initial "ll" had best be attempted only by the Welsh. Laugharne (also spelled Lacharn) has only one syllable, "larn."

Sources of Quotations

1. Dylan Thomas, "Reminiscences of Childhood" and "Return Journey," Quite Early One Morning, pp. 13–14, 89.
2. Mervyn Levy, "A Womb with a View," John O'London's (Nov. 29, 1962), p. 485.
3. Daniel Jones, "Dylan Thomas: Memories and Appreciations," Encounter (January, 1954), p. 9.
4. Dylan Thomas, "Return Journey," Quite Early One Morning, pp. 86–87.
5. Daniel Jones, "Dylan Thomas: Memories and Appreciations," Encounter (January, 1954), pp. 9–10.
6. Dylan Thomas, "Return Journey," Quite Early One Morning, p. 84.
7. Ibid., p. 71.
8. South Wales Post, June 2, 1931, as quoted in Maud and Davies (eds.), The Colour of Saying, p. xiii.
9. Dylan Thomas, as quoted in ibid., p. xiv.
10. A. E. Trick in a letter to the author.
11. Ibid.
12. Grammar School Magazine (April, 1931), as quoted by Ethel Ross, "Dylan Thomas and the Amateur Theatre," The Swan: Magazine of the Swansea Training College (March, 1958), p. 16.
13. J. D. Williams, as quoted in ibid., p. 19.
14. Ibid.
15. Pamela Hansford Johnson, "Memoir," Adam International Review (No. 238, 1953), p. 24.
16. Runia Sheila MacLeod, "The Dylan I Knew," Adam International Review (No. 238, 1953), p. 21.
17. Ibid., p. 23.
18. A. E. Trick in a letter to the author.
19. Dylan Thomas, "A Painter's Studio," Texas Quarterly (Winter, 1961), pp. 56–57.
20. Mervyn Levy, "A Womb with a View," John O'London's (Nov. 29, 1962), p. 485.
21. Rayner Heppenstall, review of 18 Poems, Adelphi (Feb., 1935), pp. 314–15.
22. Edwin Muir, review of 18 Poems, The Listener (Feb. 27, 1935). p. 381.
23. Geoffrey Grigson, review of 18 Poems, New Verse (Feb., 1935), p. 22.
24. Edith Sitwell, "Four New Poets," London Mercury (Feb., 1936), p. 388.

25. Geoffrey Grigson, "Recollections of Dylan Thomas," London Magazine (Sept., 1957), p. 41.

26. Ibid., p. 44.

27. Dylan Thomas, letter of Oct. 25, 1937, Letters to Vernon Watkins, p. 29.

28. Letter of Feb., 1939, ibid., p. 57.

29. Dylan Thomas, "Letters to Lawrence Durrell, Two Cities (May 15, 1960), p. 2.

30. Dylan Thomas, letter of April 20, 1936, Letters to Vernon Watkins, p. 23.

31. Ibid., p. 12.

32. Ibid., p. 16.

33. Review of Twenty-Five Poems, Times Literary Supplement (Sept. 19, 1936), p. 750.

34. Caitlin Thomas, Leftover Life to Kill, p. 55.

35. Rhys Davies, "Portrait of the Artist," Life and Letters Today (March, 1940), p. 338.

36. Dylan Thomas, letter of Nov. 2, 1939, to Rayner Heppenstall, Four Absentees, p. 150.

37. Dylan Thomas, letter of 1940, Letters to Vernon Watkins, p. 98.

38. Ibid., p. 99.

39. Dylan Thomas, "Our Country," Documentary News Letter (Vol. 5, 1944), p. 96.

40. Dylan Thomas, letter of March 28, 1945, "Seven Letters to Oscar Williams," New World Writing No. 7 (April, 1955), p. 129.

41. Ralph Maud, Entrances to Dylan Thomas' Poetry, p. 5.

42. Denis Botterill, review of Deaths and Entrances, Life and Letters (Nov., 1946), p. 93.

43. Dylan Thomas, letter of Aug. 26, 1946, Letters to Vernon Watkins, p. 135.

44. John Arlott, "Dylan Thomas and Radio," Adelphi (Vol. 30, No. 2 [1954]), p. 123.

45. Louis MacNeice, "Dylan Thomas: Memories and Appreciations," Encounter (Jan., 1954), p. 12.

46. Roy Campbell, "Memories of Dylan Thomas at the B.B.C.," Poetry (Nov., 1955), p. 113.

47. Dylan Thomas, letter of March 21, 1938, Letters to Vernon Watkins, p. 37.

48. Caitlin Thomas, Leftover Life to Kill, pp. 57, 64.

49. Dylan Thomas, quoted by Miron Grindea, "Memoir," Adam International Review (No. 238, 1953), p. 25.

50. Mario Luzi, "Memoir," Adam International Review (No. 238, 1953), p. 25.

51. Augusto Livi, quoted in Roberto Sanesi, Dylan Thomas, p. 132.

52. Jan Read, an unpublished preface for The Beach of Falesá.

53. Dylan Thomas, letter to Elizabeth Lutyens, "Oh Weep for Adonais," Adam International Review (No. 236, 1953), p. 3.

54. Cordelia Locke in a letter to the author.

55. Caitlin Thomas, Leftover Life to Kill, p. 34.

56. Dylan Thomas, "The Cost of Letters," Horizon (Sept. 1946), p. 174.

57. Caitlin Thomas, Leftover Life to Kill, p. 64.

58. Jack Lindsay in a letter to the author.

59. Dylan Thomas, "The Cost of Letters," Horizon (Sept., 1946), p. 175.

60. Dylan Thomas, letter of March 28, 1945, "Seven Letters to Oscar Williams," New World Writing No. 7 (April, 1955), p. 129.

61. Dylan Thomas, in a letter to John Malcolm Brinnin, Dylan Thomas in America, pp. 31–32.

62. Ibid., pp. 52–53.

63. Dylan Thomas, letter of March 25, 1951, "Seven Letters to Oscar Williams," New World Writing No. 7 (April, 1955), p. 135.

64. Dylan Thomas, in a letter to John Malcolm Brinnin, Dylan Thomas in America, p. 97.

65. Dylan Thomas, letter of May 28, 1951, "Seven Letters to Oscar Williams," New World Writing No. 7 (April, 1955), p. 136.

66. Dylan Thomas, quoted by Vernon Watkins, "Elegy," Encounter (Feb., 1956), p. 31.

67. Dylan Thomas, letter of Dec. 3, 1951, to John Malcolm Brinnin, Dylan Thomas in America, p. 131.

68. Caitlin Thomas, Leftover Life to Kill, p. 73.

69. E. F. Bozman, "Dylan Thomas," Books (Dec., 1953), pp. 114–15.

70. Dylan Thomas, letter of Nov. 6, 1952, to Marguerite Caetani, "Three Letters," Botteghe Oscure (XIII, 1954), pp. 97–100.

71. Daniel Jones, preface, Under Milk Wood, p. ix.

72. John Malcolm Brinnin, Dylan Thomas in America, p. 208.

73. Ibid., p. 216.

74. Ibid., pp. 249, 252, 271.

Bibliography
Books by Dylan Thomas

1. 18 Poems. London: The Sunday Referee and the Parton Press, 1934.
2. Twenty-Five Poems. London: J. M. Dent & Sons, 1936.
3. The Map of Love. London: J. M. Dent & Sons, 1939.
4. The World I Breathe. Norfolk, Conn.: New Directions, 1939.
5. Portrait of the Artist as a Young Dog. London: J. M. Dent & Sons, 1940.
6. New Poems. Norfolk, Conn.: New Directions, 1943.
7. Deaths and Entrances. London: J. M. Dent & Sons, 1946.
8. Selected Writings of Dylan Thomas. New York: New Directions, 1946.
9. Twenty-Six Poems. London: J. M. Dent & Sons, 1950.
10. In Country Sleep. New York: New Directions, 1952.
11. Collected Poems, 1934–1952. London: J. M. Dent & Sons, 1952.
12. The Doctor and the Devils. London: J. M. Dent & Sons, 1953.
13. Under Milk Wood. London: J. M. Dent & Sons, 1954.
14. Quite Early One Morning, Broadcasts. London: J. M. Dent & Sons, 1954.
15. Adventures in the Skin Trade and Other Stories. New York: New Directions, 1955.
16. A Prospect of the Sea. London: J. M. Dent & Sons, 1955.
17. A Child's Christmas in Wales. Norfolk, Conn.: New Directions, 1955.
18. Letters to Vernon Watkins. London: J. M. Dent & Sons and Faber & Faber, 1957.
19. The Beach of Falesá. New York: Stein & Day, 1963.

Books about Dylan Thomas

1. Henry Treece, Dylan Thomas: Dog Among the Fairies. London: Lindsay Drummond, 1949. Revised edition, London: Ernest Benn, 1959.
2. Elder Olson, The Poetry of Dylan Thomas. Chicago: University of Chicago Press, 1954.
3. Derek Stanford, Dylan Thomas. London: Neville Spearman, 1954.
4. John Malcolm Brinnin, Dylan Thomas in America. Boston: Little, Brown and Co., 1955.
5. J. Alexander Rolph, Dylan Thomas: A Bibliography. London: J. M. Dent & Sons, 1956.

6. G. S. Fraser, Dylan Thomas. London: Longmans, Green & Co., 1957.

7. Caitlin Thomas, Leftover Life to Kill. London: Putnam and Co., 1957.

8. Lita R. Hornick, The Intricate Image: A Study of Dylan Thomas. Ann Arbor, Mich.; University Microfilms Xerox Book, 1958.

9. E. W. Tedlock (ed.), Dylan Thomas: The Legend and the Poet. London: William Heinemann, 1960.

10. John Malcolm Brinnin (ed.), A Casebook on Dylan Thomas. New York: Thomas Y. Crowell, 1960.

11. Roberto Sanesi, Dylan Thomas. Milan: Lerici Editori, 1960.

12. Dieter Kappus, Die Dichterische Entwicklung von Dylan Thomas. Freiburg: Albert Ludwigs University Dissertation, 1960.

13. Rayner Heppenstall, Four Absentees. London: Barrie and Rockliff, 1960.

14. David Holbrook, Llareggub Revisited: Dylan Thomas and the State of Modern Poetry. London: Bowes & Bowes, 1962.

15. W. Y. Tindall, A Reader's Guide to Dylan Thomas. New York: Farrar, Straus and Cudahy, 1962.

16. Hélène Bokanowski and Marc Alyn, Dylan Thomas. Paris: P. Seghers, 1962.

17. Clark M. Emery, The World of Dylan Thomas. Coral Gables, Fla.: University of Miami Press, 1962.

18. William T. Moynihan, The Poetry of Dylan Thomas: a Study of its Meaning and Unity. Ann Arbor, Mich.: University Microfilms Xerox Book, 1962.

19. Thelma L. B. Murdy, Sound and Meaning in Dylan Thomas's Poetry. Ann Arbor, Mich.: University Microfilms Xerox Book, 1962.

20. T. H. Jones, Dylan Thomas. Edinburgh and London: Oliver & Boyd, 1963.

21. Ralph Maud, Entrances to Dylan Thomas' Poetry. Pittsburgh, Pa.: University of Pittsburgh Press, 1963.

22. Ralph Maud and Aneirin T. Davies (eds.), The Colour of Saying: An Anthology of Verse Spoken by Dylan Thomas. London: J. M. Dent & Sons, 1963.

23. George J. Firmage and Oscar Williams (eds.), A Garland for Dylan Thomas. New York: Clarke & Way, 1963.

24. Hyman H. Kleinman, The Religious Sonnets of Dylan Thomas: A Study in Imagery and Meaning. Berkeley: University of California Press, 1963.

25. Aneirin T. Davies, Dylan: Druid of the Broken Body. London: J. M. Dent & Sons, 1964.
26. Sidney Michaels, Dylan. New York: Random House, 1964.

Index

A

Abraham Lincoln 50
Ackland, Rodney 52
Adelphi 63, 76, 84
Adventures in the Skin Trade 167
Aeschylus 116
"After the Fair" 53, 82
"After the Funeral" 45
Agamemnon 116
Aldington, Richard 29
Algren, Nelson 140
Alwyn, William 104
"And Death Shall Have No Dominion"
  53
Anglo-Iranian Oil Co. 144
Apollinaire 133
Archer, David 65
Arlott, John 115
Athraw, Yr 21
Auden, W. H. 53, 58, 96, 139
Aumonier, Stacy 29
Austen, Jane 87
Ayrton, Michael 122

B

"Balloon Site 568" 104
"Bandalero" 76
Bard's Eye View of the United States,
  A 156
Barker, George 144
Barnes, George 119
Barrie, J. M. 50
Beach of Falesá, The 127
Beaux' Strategem, The 51
Beckett, Samuel 96
Beddoes, T. L. 57
Berkeley, Lennox 102
Berti, Luigi 123
Best Poems of the Year 58
Bigongiari, Piero 123-4
Blake, William 57, 117
Blakeston, Oswell 81
Boccaporto 123
Bookman 63
Book of Verse 115
Booster 91
Botteghe Oscure 146, 149
Botterill, Denis 113
Box, Sydney 127
Boyle, Kay 96
Boys, Henry 102
Boys' Own Paper 45
Bozman, E. F. 155
Brancusi, Constantin 80
Breton, André 82, 133
Brinnin, Mrs. Frances 153
Brinnin, John Malcolm 137, 140, 144,
  152, 160, 163-7
British Broadcasting Corporation 63,
  102, 107, 115-19, 128, 133, 144, 149,
  156, 160
British Petroleum Co. 144
Brooke, Rupert 29
Browning, Robert 29
"Burning Baby, The" 62
Burning Baby, The 96, 98, 100
Burns, Robert 106
Byron, Lord 57

C

Caedmon 153
Caetani, Marguerite 146, 152, 156
Caldwell, Erskine 96
Caldwell, Sarah 166
Cambria Daily Leader 28
Cameron, Norman 78, 81, 122, 134

Campbell, Roy 116-7, 144
Capek, Karel 50
Caravel 81
Carr, John Dickson 96
Cartier-Bresson, Henri 146
Carswell, Catherine 106
"Ceremony After a Fire Raid" 136
Cervantes, Miguel 119
Chaplin, Charles 140-1
Charlie, Bonnie Prince 79
Chaucer, Geoffrey 57
Child's Christmas in Wales, A 119
Choate, Dean Robert A. 166
Christian Agitator, The 45
Christie, Agatha 96
Churchill, Winston 53
Collected Poems 113, 153, 155
Columbus 103
Combs, Tram 140
Comment 81, 84
Communist Party 134
Congreve, William 52
Connolly, Cyril 80
Contemporary Poetry and Prose 84, 96
"Conversation About Christmas" 119
Cooke, Arnold 102
Cooper, Sir Alfred 84
Cooper, Susanna 85
"Cost of Letters, The" 132
"Council for the Encouragement of
  Music and Art" 104
"Country Comes to the Town, The"
  103
Cour, Ronald 34
Coward, Noel 50
Crane, Stephen 58
Criterion 84
Cummings, E. E. 141

D

Daily Worker, The 136
Dali, Salvador 82
Davenport, John 102, 104, 122, 175
Davies, Aneirin Talfan 116, 119, 173,
  175
"Dawn in Britain, The" 116
Death of the King's Canary, The 102
Deaths and Entrances 113
Death's Jest Book 57
de la Mare, Walter 29, 58
Delta 91
Dent, J. M. 79, 84, 95, 146
"Desert Idyll" 51
Devas, Anthony 85
Devas, Nicolette Macnamara 85, 175
Devlin, Denis 96
Dickinson, Patric 116
Doctor and the Devils, The 106, 156
Documentary News Letter 104
"Do Not Go Gentle into That Good
  Night" 149-50
Dos Passos, John 96
Doughty, Charles M. 116
Drinkwater, John 50
Dryden, J. 117
Duncan, Isadora 85
Durrell, Lawrence 91
Dyall, Franklin 62
Dylan Thomas in America 139

E

Eberhart, Mignon 96
18 Poems 45, 53, 76, 78
Eisenhower, Gen. D. D. 141
Eldridge, John 104, 107
Eliot, T. S. 55, 58, 62, 81, 96

Eluard, Paul 82, 96
Empson, William 81, 102
"End of the River, The" 53
Escape 51
"Especially When the October Wind'
  65
Europa Press 96
Ewart, Gavin 134

F

Faber and Faber 65
Farquhar, George 51
Farr, Fred 38, 40
Feltenstein, Dr. Milton 173
Ferguson, Mrs. 28
Ferlinghetti, Lawrence 140
"Fern Hill" 24, 175
"Fight, The" 29
Film Pictorial 59
Fisher, Fanya 107
"Force that Through the Green Fuse,
  The" 45, 54
Ford, Charles Henri 96
Forster, E. M. 58
"Foster the Light" 65
Frankenberg, Lloyd 141, 153

G

Gainsborough Films 127
Galsworthy, John 50-1, 58
García Lorca, Federigo 100
Gardner, Erle Stanley 96
Garrigue, Jean 141
Gascoyne, David 54, 66, 82, 134
Gauguin, Paul 60-1, 74
"Genius and Madness Akin in World
  of Art" 41
Georgian Anthology 58
Glock, William 102
Golding, Louis 101
Goldman, Jeanne Gordon 141
Goodridge, Doreen 52
Goulden, Mark 65
Graves, Robert 76
"Greek Play in a Garden" 41
Greene, Graham 104
"Grief Ago, A" 78
Grierson, John 103
Grigson, Geoffrey 62, 65, 76-81, 96,
  134
Grimm 59
Gryphon Films 128
Guggenheim, Peggy 81

H

Hannum, Herb 170
Hardy, Thomas 139
Harris, Frank 146
Harris, E. Howard 41
Hay Fever 50-2
Haypetrie 106
Henderson, Mrs. Wyn 81-2, 87
Heppenstall, Rayner 76, 100
Herald of Wales 38, 41
Herbert, George 59
Higham, David 98
"His Requiem" 29, 45
Hitler, Adolf 53
Holdridge, Barbara 153
Hole, Mrs. 26
Hook, Half 38
Hopkins, Gerard Manley 29, 58, 117
Hopkins, Mrs. 129
Horizon 102, 132, 136
"Houdini" 170
Housman, Lawrence 50

Howson, Mrs. 62
"How Soon the Servant Sun" 95
Hubbard, Anthony 75
Hughes, Eric 38, 50-1
Hughes, Gareth 38
Hughes, Richard 84, 101
Hughes, Trevor 42, 76
"Hunchback in the Park, The" 44-5
Hutchinson 117
Huxley, Aldous 58

I

"I, in My Intricate Image" 113
Imagist Anthology 58
"I Make This in a Warring Absence" 87
Imperial Chemical Industries 104
"In Country Sleep" 125
In Country Sleep 153
"In My Craft and Sullen Art" 153
"In the Direction of the Beginning" 87
"In the White Giant's Thigh" 144
Inventario 123
"I See the Boys of Summer" 45
Isherwood, Christopher 140
"Is Your Ernie Really Necessary?" 106
"Is Your Journey Really Necessary"
  106

J

James, Henry 57
Janes, Fred 47, 70-5, 82, 95, 175
Janus 84
Jennings, John 76
John, Augustus 84, 87, 96, 98, 134
John, Vivian 85
John O'London's 67
Johnson, Amy Clothilda 60-2, 96
Johnson, Pamela Hansford 54-71, 102,
  113, 122, 134
Jones, Ann 24, 87, 90-1
Jones, Daniel Jenkin 29, 32-4, 70, 79,
  163, 175
Jones, James 24
Jones, Parry 122
Joyce, James 58, 100

K

Kafka, Franz 96, 134
Kazin, Pearl 141
Keats, John 57
Keene, Ralph 103, 127
Kent, Rockwell 79

L

"Lament" 149
Landor, W. S. 41
Lane, Rose Wilder 96
Latham, William 38
Laughlin, James 98, 115, 139
Lawrence, D. H. 29, 58, 139
Lawrite, John 117
Leftover Life to Kill 123
Levy, Mervyn 28, 72-6
Lewis, Alun 139
Lewis, Cecil Day 53, 101
Life and Letters Today 81, 84, 100, 113
"Life and the Modern Poet" 115
Life of Robert Burns 106
"Light Breaks Where No Sun Shines"
  62, 115
Lindsay, Jack 134
Lindsay, Philip 104
Listener, The 62, 76, 115
Livi, Augusto 125
Llareggub 50, 152, 156, 160

Llewelyn, Richard 101
Locke, Cordelia and Harry 129
Locke, Nicola 129
London Library of Recorded English 153
London Mercury 58, 78
Lougee, David 141
Lowery, Glyn 38
Lutyens, Elisabeth 128
Luzi, Mario 123-4
Lye, Jane and Len 139

M

Mabinogion 55
Macbeth 57
MacDiarmid, Hugh 134
MacIver, Loren 141, 152
McKenna, Rosalie Thorne 152, 163, 167
MacLeod, Runia Sheila 54, 65-6
Macnamara, Brigit, Marnier 85
Macnamara, Caitlin 84-90
Macnamara, Francis 84-5
Macnamara, John 85
Macnamara, Nicolette, Devas, 85, 175
Macnamara, Yvonne Majolier 85-90, 175
MacNeice, Louis 53, 116, 139, 175
Majolier, Edouard 85
Mantell, Marianne 153
Map of Love, The 45, 84, 87, 90, 98, 100
Marles, Gwilym 21-2
Marnier, Brigit Macnamara 123
Marnier, Tobias 123
Marquand, J. P. 96
Marionettes 84
Marsh, Ngaio 96
Marx Brothers 58, 75
Massachusetts Institute of Technology 153
Masters, Edgar Lee 156
"Matthew Passion, The" 82
Maugham, Somerset 100
Me and My Bike 127-8
"Memories of Christmas" 119
Merchant of Venice, The 62
Millay, Edna St. Vincent 58
Miller, Henry 91-2, 98
Milton, John 66, 124
Ministry of Information 104, 106
"Minor Poets of Old Swansea" 41
Mitchell, Oswald 106
"Modern Poet of Gower: Mr. E. Howard Harris, A" 41
Moffat, Curtis and Ivan 103
Monro, Harold 58
Montale, Eugenio 123-4
Moore, George 87
Moore, Henry 82, 101
Moore, Marianne 146
Morris, Sir Lewis 116
Morton 136
Moss, Stanley 141
Muir, Edwin 76
Murray, Gilbert 58
Mussolini, Benito 53

N

Nash, Paul 82
"Nellie Wallace's Mimicry" 35
Neuburg, Benjamin Victor 54-5, 65-6
New Directions 98, 100, 146, 153
New English Weekly 53, 84, 87, 96

Newlands, Bert 128
New Outlook 45
New Stories 84
"New Towns for Old" 104
New Verse 62, 65, 76-8, 95, 134
Nezval, Vitezslav 133-4
Nineties Anthology 58
No Room at the Inn 128
"Now Say Nay" 95

O

Obelisk Press 98
O'Brien, Flann 96
O'Casey, Sean 62
"Ode on St. Cecilia's Day" 117
Odyssey 128
Office of War Information 106
"Old Garbo" 38
Oliver Cromwell 51
"O Make Me a Mask" 87
"Once It Was the Colour of Saying" 98
Orage, A. R. 53
Osbiston, Alan 104
O'Sullivan, Maurice 106
"Our Country" 104
Our Time 136
Out of Bounds 136
"Out of the Pit" 53
"Out of the Sighs" 44
Overseas Service 115
Owen, Wilfred 58
Oxford Book of Welsh Verse 22

P

Paradise Lost 116
Parker, Dorothy 96
Parronchi, Alessandro 123-4
Parton Bookshop 65
Patchen, Kenneth 140
Patmore, Coventry 116
Peacock, Thomas Love 153
Pearn, Pollinger, and Higham 98
Penrose, Roland 82
Peter and Paul 51
Petronius 116
Pleasure Dome 153
Plomer, William 63
Pocock, Robert 175
"Poem in the Ninth Month" 98
"Poem in October" 109, 115, 153
"Poem on His Birthday" 149
"Poet, 1935" 41
"Poets' Corner, The" 54, 72
"Poets of Swansea" 41
Pope, Alexander 117
"Pornography in Nineteenth Century Literature" 67
Porteous, Hugh 81
Portrait of the Artist as a Young Dog, A 42, 100, 103
Post, The London 78, 81, 96
Post, South Wales Daily 35, 38, 41, 51
Powell, Michael 128
Powys, J. C. 87
Preston, Hayter 54
Prichard, John 95, 175
Prichard, Llewelyn 41
Priestley, J. B. 101
Programme 78, 81
Prokosch, Frederic 96
"Prologue to an Adventure" 42
Prophetic Books, The 57
Prose and Verse 41-2
Prydyddiaeth 22
Purpose 81

Q

"Quite Early One Morning" 107, 160
Quite Early One Morning 119

R

"Rake's Progress, The" 166
Rank, J. Arthur 127
Rau, Santha Rama 173
Read, Herbert 82, 101
Read, Jan 127
Reavey, George 96, 98
Rebecca's Daughters 127
Rees, David 22, 24, 41
Reitell, Elizabeth 163, 170
"Religio Laici" 117
Religious Tract Society 98
"Return Journey" 31, 119
Rexroth, Kenneth 140
Rhys, Keidrych 42, 175
Richard II 52
Rickword, Edgell 134
Roethke, Theodore 141
Rodgers, W. R. 144
Roosevelt, F. D. 53
Rosai, Ottone 123-4
Rosenbergs 137
Ross, Ethel 51
Rossetti, Christina 57
Rota, Bertram 146
Rotha, Paul 103
Rouault, Georges 146
Roughton, Roger 96
Rubinstein, H. F. 51

S

"Sacre du Printemps, Le" 167
"Saint About to Fall, A" 98
Saintsbury, George 57
Sandburg, Carl 141
Sassoon, Siegfried 58
Satyricon 116
Sayers, Dorothy 96
Scottish Bookman 81
Scott, William 78, 82
Searle, Humphrey 102
Selected Writings 115
Seven 84
Shakespeare 29, 116, 124
Shaw, G. B. 50, 58
Shelley, P. B. 57
Sitwell, Edith 58, 78, 80, 139, 146
Sitwell, Osbert 58
Sitwell, Sacheverell 29, 58
Skoumal, Aloys 133
Slivka, David and Rose 153
Smaller Rose Garden, The 133
Socialist Party 45, 136
Sommerfield, John 134
"Song of Ceylon" 103
"Song of the Mischievous Dog" 29
Spencer, Bernard 78, 95
Spender, Stephen 53, 62-3, 101, 124,
  159
"Spire Cranes, The" 44, 87
Stalin, Josef 139
Stein, Gertrude 87
Stevenson, R. L. 127
Stewart, Gordon 70
Stockholm Peace Petition 136
"Story of Llewelyn Prichard, The" 41
"Story of Paraclete, The" 41
Stout, Rex 96
Strand Films 103, 106
Strange Orchestra 52
Stratford Film Co. 128

Stravinsky, Igor 128, 166
Strife 51
Struwelpeter 26
Studio, The 82
Summersbee, Col. 60
Sunday Referee 54, 63, 65, 72
Sunday Times 78
Surrealist Exhibition 82
Swansea and West Wales Guardian 45,
  136
Swansea Grammar School Magazine
  29, 34, 50
Swift, Jonathan 133
Swingler, Randall 134
Symphony for Full Orchestra 58, 63

T

Taig, Thomas 47
"Tales of Mystery and Imagination" 48
Taylor, A. J. P. 125
Taylor, Donald 103, 106-9, 113
Taylor, Frank 141
Taylor, Haydn 50, 60
Taylor, Margaret 125, 132, 146, 175
Telegraph, Morning 59
Temple, Shirley 98
Tennyson, Alfred 63
"That Modern Youth is Decadent" 51
"That Sanity Be Kept" 54-5
"These Are the Men" 104
Third Programme 117, 119
This Bed Thy Centre 65
"This is Colour" 104
Thomas, Aeron 106, 129, 156
Thomas, Arthur 22
Thomas, Colm Garan 132, 159, 170
Thomas, David John 22, 34, 55, 63,
  92, 104, 127, 129, 132, 149
Thomas, Edward 146
Thomas, Evan 22
Thomas, Florence Williams 55, 92, 129,
  132, 175
Thomas, Llewelyn Edouard 98, 102,
  129, 156
Thomas, Nancy, Taylor Summersbee
  24, 50, 55, 60, 175
Thomas, William (Gwilym Marles) 21-2
Thomas, William (brother of D. J.) 22
Thomas, Wynford Vaughan 35
Thorns of Thunder, The 96
Three Weird Sisters 128
"Three Wise Men of Gotham, The" 153
Thunderer, The 34
Times, London 63, 95
"Today This Insect and the World I
  Breathe" 44
Todd, Ruthven 78, 96, 139, 170
Town That was Mad, The 163
Toynbee, Philip 155
"Tragedy of Swansea's Comic Genius"
  41
Transition 84
Tree, Iris 103
Tregaskis, Beth 66
"Tribute to Auden" 87
Trick, Albert E. 45-50, 53, 67, 74, 76,
  81, 101, 136, 160
Trick, Nell and Pamela 47-8, 50
"Trimalchio's Feast" 116
Turgenev 87
Twenty-Five Poems 45, 78, 95, 103
Twenty-Six Poems 144
Twenty Years A-Growing 106
Two Dogs 119
Two Streets 164

U

Under Milk Wood 50, 107, 160-4, 167, 170

V

Valentino, Rudolph 51
Van Dine, S. S. 96
Van Gogh, Vincent 74
Vanity Fair 128
"Verse of James Chapman Wood" 41
"Visit to Grandpa's, A" 53

W

Wales 42, 84, 104
Wales, University College of 22, 47
Wallace, Nellie 35, 38
Walpole, Hugh 101
Ward, Dan and Rose 79, 81
Warner, Tom 47, 95
"War Song of Dinas Vawr, The" 153
Watkins, Vernon 90, 92-5, 102, 146, 149, 175
Watson, Peter 101
Way of the World, The 52, 58
Wells, H. G. 96, 101
Welsh Home Service 119
"We Lying by Seasand" 87
Western Counties Gazette 45
Western Mail 29, 45
WGBH 153
Whips and Scorpions 58
White, Antonia 102
Whittier, J. G. 29

"Why East Wind Chills" 44
Wickham, Anna 91
Wilder, Thornton 141
Williams, Cliff 38
Williams, Elizabeth Mary 22
Williams, Florence 22
Williams, Ivy and Ebbie 175
Williams, J. D. 51
Williams, Rev. J. R. 175
Williams, Oscar 137
Williams, S. B. 175
Williams, Ted 40
Williams, Theodosia 22, 24
Williams, Tom 24
Williams, William Carlos 96
Winters, Shelley 140-1
Within the Gates 62
Witt-Diamant, Ruth 140
Wodehouse, P. G. 87
Wolfe, Humbert 58
Woods, James Chapman 41
Woolf, Virginia 58
Wordsworth, William 57
World I Breathe, The 100
Wright, Basil 103

Y

Yeats, W. B. 29, 58, 139
Yellow Jacket 84
Ymofynydd, Yr 22
Young Men's Hebrew Association 137, 153, 163, 170
"Youth Calls to Age" 41